Factors that Determine Entrepreneurial Behaviour in
Micro and Small Enterprises (MSEs)
in Kenya

Isaac Mokaya Maragia

Nsemia

First Edition: October 2014
Published by Nsemia Inc. Publishers, Oakville, Ontario, Canada (www. nsemia.com)

Cover Concept Illustration: Isaac Mokaya Maragia
Cover Design: Danielle Pitt
Layout Design: Truphena Matunda

Note for Librarians:
A cataloguing record for this book is available From Library and Archives Canada.

ISBN: 978-1-926906-35-5 Paperback
Previously (2008) Issued as ISBN: 9966-909-76-1

DEDICATION

This book is dedicated to the entrepreneurs who touched my life and that of many others: my parents, Mzee Joseph Maragia Ongeri and Mama Rodha Kemunto; John Obae, Z. Nyatera, Mzee Pastor Johnstone Agoki omenge, the late Mwalimu Peter Ongeri Maragia, the late Kefa Maragia, Benjamin Kiriago, all my brothers and sisters, Aunt mong'ina from whom I learnt some initial entrepreneurial lessons; and my dear family, Lady Jane, Peter Nyakundi and Jerusha Nyanchoka. Their patience and understanding contributed immensely to the successful completion of this work.

CONTENTS

CHAPTER ONE
THE ENTREPRENEUR AND
ENTREPRENEURSHIP

CHAPTER TWO
CASE STUDY OF KARIOBANGI LIGHT INDUSTRIES

CHAPTER THREE
DATA ANALYSIS AND FINDINGS

CHAPTER FOUR
DISCUSSION AND CONCLUSION

APPENDICES

ACKNOWLEDGEMENTS

I received a lot of support and encouragement in completing this work. I am particularly in debt to Prof. Henry Bwisa for his special attention and critical supervision during our numerous meetings at the University of Nairobi where I got the insight into the concept of entrepreneurship and small business development.

I thank my advisor. Dr. Michael Busler for guiding the study projects. Further gratitude to Lady Jane Maragia and our children, Peter Lesley Ongeri Nyakundi Maragia and Jerusha Mongina Nyanchoka Maragia, for being so supportive as to wake me up at odd hours of the night and very early mornings to do readings for this work. Their support went along way to challenge and motivate me whenever I felt like giving up.

I am also grateful to Prof. Dorothy McCormick for her motivation and keen interest in my pursuit of scholarly investigation of entrepreneurial behaviour in Kenya, specifically of micro and small enterprises. Prof. McCormick allowed me to use her own library during my study of literature on the subject.

I benefited immensely from the scholarly advice of Dr. Enock Kinara, Prof. P.O. Berg of Lund University, Sweden, Prof. Isaac Meroka Mbeche, Principal of the College of Humanities, University of Nairobi, Prof. Aosa, Prof. Kibera, Prof. G.P. Pokhariyal (for statistics insights and academic curiosity), Prof. Kulundu, Prof. P.O. K'Obonyo, John Omiti, PhD, of the Institute of Policy Analysis and Research, Mr. Machuka of treasury, Kenya, Prof. Japheth Maranga, Prof. N Nyaundi and Mrs. Alice Nyaundi.

Special thanks to Mr. Levis Mutsetse for questionnaire construction and academic critique and the numerous meetings at which we discussed strategies for the success of this project. I am grateful to Mr. Kisaka Sifunjo for data analysis on SPSS.

I thank the staff at Washington International University for their timely communications, feedback and quick responses to queries.

I am indebted to Prof. George Agoki and Dr.Philip Mainda, Isaiah Makana, Cyrus Omesa, James Gesumwa and Modekai Ochieng for inviting me to visit United States of America where I got access to Andrews University library for research material that was not easily available in Kenya. The international journals at the university proved quite useful.

I am greatly indebted to fellow doctoral students at university of Nairobi: Dr. Martin Odipo, Fred Chune, Lady Beatrice Sabana, CEO Micro

Finance Institution Association, Edward Odundo, Dr. Kipngetich, Director KWS, David Nyameino, Mr.Ntale, Dr. Charles K.Okioga, Mr. Okiri Mochache, Mr.Cliff Mainda, Dr.Awino, Mr.Fred Nyakweba, Patrick Chogo, Ken Nyasinga, Steve Omenge, Hobson Onsomu and Joan Ondari.

I am equally indebted to the management of Kenya Revenue Authority for Financial support and a progressive training policy that encouraged me to face the daunting challenge of doctoral training. Special thanks to the Commissioner General, Mr. M.G.Waweru.

I wish to make special mention of Mr.Michael Onyula, P.B.O Odeny, G.Obbayi, J.G Ndegwa, Sophie Abuga, Mose, David Obure, S.C. Wafula, Mary Kiriago and family members and F.Asin who often lifted my spirits when the going got tough. Commissioner Kepha Ole Tande made it possible for me to pursue coursework at university of Nairobi. I am greatly humbled by his support.

Colleagues at work provided much encouragement: Mr. Stanley Mutugi, Nyambaka, Ombasa, Stanley Mugetha, TOT Team, Principal Analo of KRAT, Serem, Winnie, Electronic Tax Register Team (ETR) to Italy and Greece, comprising Mr. Tekye of Petken ltd, Mrs. Beatrice Nyongesa, Mr. Tobias K'Onyango, and JT Ngugi treasury for your contribution to my comfort.

I received special support from Hon. Justice E.S.O. Bosire and Hon. Henry Obwacha, former minister for economic planning, Kenya.

I also thank the Kakamega/Bungoma office team of Agnes Mbungu B.K. Cheruiyot and all staff members for your invaluable support.

The financial assistance of the Higher Education Loans Board (HELB) is acknowledged and appreciated. Finally yet importantly, I am immensely grateful to my brothers and sisters. You are also special.

There are other many people who I cannot mention by name but whose support and prayers were critical to the success of this book.

Thank you

Finally, glory be to God Almighty of his divine grace was sufficient all the time. Amen.

ABBREVIATIONS

AMKIM   Associate Member Kenya Institute of management

BBC   British Broadcasting Corporation

BDS   Business Development Services

CBD   Central Business District

CDR   Centre for Development Research

CEO   Chief Executive Officer

DNA   Deoxyribonucleic Acid

Etc   Etcetera

G.D.P   Gross Domestic Product

GOK   Government of Kenya

ILO   International Labour Organization

IBM   International Business Machine

ICEG   International Center for Economic Growth

IDS   Institute of Development Research

KICC   Kenya International Conference Centre

KLI   Kariobangi Light Industries

MD   Managing Director

MFI (s) Micro Finance Institutions

MMSE   Micro Medium and Small Enterprises

MPM   Master in Personal Management

MSEs   Micro and Small Enterprises

NGO   Non-Governmental Organization

NSSF   National Social Security Fund

OECD   Organization for Economic Cooperation and
         Development

PC   Personal Computers

PhD	Doctor of Philosophy
PP	Pages
Prof	Professor
SACCO	Savings and Credit Cooperative Societies
SBA	Small Business Administration
SPSS	Statistical Program for Social Sciences
U.S.A	United States of America
UK	United Kingdom
UNDP	United Nations Development Programme
VAT	Value Added Tax

COMMENTARY

This book examines the factors that determine entrepreneurial behaviour in Micro and Small Enterprises (MSEs) in Kenya. MSEs have been acknowledged as an important source of livelihood, employment, and wealth creation and thus effective tools for poverty alleviation.

In conducting the research that led to this work, the author used purposive sampling to obtain a sample of 170 entrepreneurs in service sub- sectors, trading and manufacturing at Kariobangi South Light Industries (KLI) in Nairobi, Kenya. KLI hosts a large and diverse population of informal entrepreneurs. The research focused on the following areas: training, work, experience, motivation, access to resources, and government policy.

The author uses the institution framework approach to explain the position of MSE(s). In this framework, there is enormous potential and responsibility for enterprises to contribute to the national economy and society. There is evidence of perceived constraint factors within the sector. These inhibit entrepreneurial growth and survival. It was observed that a certain category of MSEs who relied on informal institutions were able to overcome some of the perceived constraints. In countries where this was achieved, such entrepreneurs had utilized resources like finance, labour, space security and communication. They held most of their awareness campaigns in churches, Mosques and temples.

However, where networks are not prevalent, especially amongst aspiring African entrepreneurs, it is much more difficult to break through to the survival stage. The failure of business in Kenya, particularly the co-operative sector and parastatals, is attributed to poor management, corruption and political interference (Rajab, 1966)[1.] Bulunywa (1988) attributes these problems to the inherited African business environment compounded by lack of access to finances, market information and lack of managerial skills. He asserts

---

1   John Rajab.(1966). "Troubles erupts in the institute co-ops, difficulties in Gusii," East African Social and Cultural Affairs, June (1966), Washington, D.C 20036, U.S.A

that there is little attention paid to MSEs, which is the underlying factor inhibiting the development of any business.

The emerging trend of business in Kenya is that MSEs will continue to be a critical source of livelihood, job and wealth creation and growth of the economy.

FOREWORD

The role of entrepreneurship and entrepreneurial culture in economic and social development cannot be overemphasized. Global research shows that entrepreneurship does indeed contribute to economic development. It has been claimed that entrepreneurship makes the difference between developed and developing nations. The latter have been said to have the low total entrepreneurial activity.

Transforming ideas into economic opportunities is the crux of entrepreneurship. History shows that economic progress has been significantly advanced by pragmatic people who are entrepreneurial and innovative, able to exploit opportunities and willing to take risks.

Private sector development and entrepreneurship development are essential ingredients for achieving the millennium development goal of reducing poverty. For many developing countries, private sector development has now been recognized as a powerful engine of economic growth and wealth creation, and crucial for improving the quality, number and variety of employment opportunities for the poor.

If all entrepreneurs are business people then not all business people are entrepreneurs. Entrepreneurs are known to start business ventures and continually strive to improve them for growth by being creative and innovate. Thus, entrepreneurs create and bring to life new technologies, products and services and create new markets and jobs along the way. They are smart, risk takers, implementers, rule-breakers or in a word, innovators.

In developing nations such as Kenya, many obstacles stand in the way of nascent and practising entrepreneurs. It is for this reason that any literature that seeks to identify factors that affect entrepreneurial behaviour must be taken with the seriousness that it deserves.

This book makes a very useful contribution to understanding the factors that affect entrepreneurial behaviour. It will add great value in the field of entrepreneurship.

Henry M Bwisa
Professor of entrepreneurship and
Chairman, Kenya Investment Authority

INTRODUCTION

The micro and small enterprises sector in Kenya has always occupied a pivotal position in the development of the economy. The sector is a primary source of employment and income. It expanded from employing 3.7 million people in 1999 to 5.1 million in 2002 according to a recent report (sessional paper No. 3 of 2004).[2]

Research has shown that the MSE concept has been known in Kenya since 1972 when the International Labour Organization (ILO) introduced it. However, it was not until 1990 that the Kenya Government formulated ways of implementing it in a much publicized nationwide campaign (Baseline survey 1999). The role of MSE in Kenya's development process is significant particularly in the context of generating employment, wealth creation and income opportunities to thousands of people across the country (Dando, 1995).[3]

The importance of MSE to the Kenyan economy cannot be emphasized. Even in the developed economies of the UK and USA, micro and small enterprises make a great contribution to employment generation and creation of wealth, invoking great interest in many governments.

A study by David Ferrand (Baumol, 1998, p.8)[4] argues that MSEs Offer a solution to the problem of employment generation and economic imbalances. The entrepreneur is a role model in a society, one who creates something new, something different, always "searching for change responding to it, and exploiting it" (Mary Coulter, 2000, p.21)[5]

The reputation of entrepreneurs from developed countries in the European Union (EU), rest of Europe and USA is remarkable. In America for instance, entrepreneurs are respected for their role in creating new jobs, providing new competition to existing businesses, improving product

2   Sessional Paper No. 3 of 2004: Development of Micro and Small Enterprises for Wealth Creation and Employment Generation. (Republic of Kenya). Ministry of Labour and Human Resources Development (2004).
3   Aleke Dando, C. (1995). The Changing Roles of Key Institutions in Implementing of Credit Programmes for Small Scale Enterprises Development in Kenya. In English and Henault (1995).
     -David, Ferrand 1998, Thesis, the Missing Middle in Kenya.
4   David Ferrand. (1998). Discontinuity in Development: Kenya's Middle Scale Manufacturing Industry, Thesis submitted for PhD, University of Durham 1998.
5   Baumol, W.J.(1990). Entrepreneurship: Productive, Unproductive and Destructive, Journal of Political Economy, 1990 Vol. 98 No,3,pp 893 – 921,The University of Chicago.

quality, reducing prices, introducing new goods and services through innovation and technology advancement. For example, Bill Gates, through Microsoft has contributed immensely towards information technology. Suffice it to say entrepreneurship has formed the basis for advancement in technology through creation of new job-markets (Baumol, 1990)[6]

The concept of micro and small enterprises (MSEs) is not new in many developing countries. According to the Kenya 1999 National Baseline Survey report, micro and small enterprises have been defined as businesses employing up to 50 workers. By employment, it does not necessarily refer merely to the payment of wages; it includes those engaged in the activities of the business. It should be noted that in Kenya, micro enterprises are businesses employing up to ten workers including the owner while small enterprises employ more than 10 and up to 50 workers (McCormick, 1996).[7]

MSEs in Kenya have grown from 910,000 in 1993 to about 1.3 million in 1999 and the number is expected to grow further, accounting for up to 74.2% of the total employment. MSE contribution to GDP increased from 13.85% in 1993 to about 18.4% in 2002 (Sessional Paper No.3 of 2004)[8].

Small enterprises started at family level have grown to contribute to national revenues by way of taxes. Small enterprises in South East Asian countries like Japan, India, Korea and China have contributed immensely towards creation of new goods and services.

Market failure has constrained MSE development in Kenya and in many developing countries in areas of access to information, finance, labour skills, and business development services (BDS) necessary for competitiveness and productivity. Lack of information and experience in transactions is a common factor that hinders the progress of MSEs

---

6 Mary Coulter, Entrepreneurship in Action (2000) Prentice Hall, Upper Saddle River, New Jersey 07458

7 Dorothy McCormick (1996) The impact of economic reform on entrepreneurial activity. A theoretical framework for analysing small enterprise, a journal of eastern African Library and Cultural studies IDS – Nairobi.

8 Republic of Kenya, Sessional Paper No.3 of 2004: Development of Micro and Small Enterprises for Wealth Creation and Employment Generation.

- Baumol, W. J. (1989). *Entrepreneurship:: Productive, Unproductive and Destructive*. Journal or Political Economy, 1990 Vol. 98 No.3 pp. 893 – 921, The University of Chicago.

towards the willingness to take risks. Nevertheless, Kenya with its long private sector tradition has significant potential to establishing sustainable support services; demand driven approaches are likely to bring forth a sustainable supply response (Bwisa, 2001, pp. 1-40)[9].

It is anticipated that if measures are put in place to ensure that MSE entrepreneurs have access to finance, the skills required to cope with market demands and market linkages, their access to resources for growth would be facilitated (sessional paper No 3 of 2004, p8)[10]. Also required in this regard are a reduction of critical investment climate constraints, helping in MSEs to exploit opportunities and overcome bottlenecks by obtaining training, preparing business plans and strategic planning and reducing the cost of compliance with business regulations.

Micro and small entrepreneurs in Kenya both men and women, have attempted to express their desire to improve and expand, but majority of them have given up; others remain stagnant or collapse. This is most likely due to deficiencies in entrepreneurial behaviour. The absences of these factors have been found to limit the capacity of individuals to comprehend their requirements in the present competitive business environment and the necessary to adopt technology – for example computers, internet and e-commerce.

However, it is important to mention that many agencies, NGOs, ILO, Government of Kenya (GOK), and the international community have tried to assist and stimulate Kenyan entrepreneurship. Nonetheless, some of the funding and technical assistance given to business people in cooperative societies in the 1980s, for example, brought little or no capacity to attain modern economic discipline and business standards. It proved futile and a waste of money and

other development resources. Indeed, it pointed to the necessity of seeking ways to develop the factors mentioned above among a critical mass of Kenyan entrepreneurs. The Kenya government would need to ascertain that if developed, these factors would lead to the desired result.

Whereas studies conducted in other countries have attributed lack of entrepreneurial dynamism to deficiency in factors that influence entrepreneurial behaviour, studies in Kenya mainly concentrate on failures of micro and small enterprises, also

9   Bwisa, H.M. (2001). "Promoting Demand Driven S and T Policy Research for Kneys's Micro Processors: A Concept Paper at National Workshop for Jua Kali Agro-Processors, ATPS and IDRC, July 2001-Nairobi.
10   Sessional Paper No. 3 of 2004: Development of Micro and Small Enterprises for Wealth and Employment Creation (GOK).

known as informal sector. However the local studies do not refute the fact that some businesses have fallen victim to failure due to other factors such as poor legal and regulatory frameworks, family business influence, gender and infrastructure. These additional factors make the Kenyan context somewhat complex and difficult; different from those of developed countries. It is therefore necessary to conduct a study in Kenya to find out the extent to which entrepreneurial behaviours are conditioned by factors, which have been practised successfully in such countries as USA, Japan, India and china. There is a pronounced lack of information about why many Kenyan entrepreneurs do not flourish in their micro and small endeavours. Available literature merely attributes this to lack of entrepreneurial skills, education and experience amongst entrepreneurs.

This book is a response to the need for credible explanations of entrepreneurial success. Briefly, it examines the extent to which selected factors (for example experience, training, formal education, innovativeness and alertness to opportunities) explain entrepreneurial orientation or behavioural response an opportunity.

The book seeks to understand the factors that determine entrepreneurial behaviour and how these factors propel the entrepreneur to start a business enterprise. Specifically it intends to:

1. Determine the factors that influence entrepreneurial behaviour amongst entrepreneurs in Kenya.
2. Contribute to the development of a theory of entrepreneurship in micro and small enterprises MSEs
3. Identify and explain the factors that dominate most entrepreneurs
4. Determine if there is lack of enterprise culture amongst Kenyans

This book is important in several respects. First, it can serve to inform government policy. Stakeholders like the donor community, micro finance institutions and NGOs will also find it beneficial. Secondly would be entrepreneurs will find the book useful in areas of training and preparation to enter entrepreneurship. Furthermore the book fills a worrying gap in theory of entrepreneurship in micro and small enterprises. Lastly, research students in the study of entrepreneurship will find the book a useful reference.

Chapter One

THE ENTREPRENEUR AND ENTREPRENEURSHIP

1.0 Introduction

The entrepreneur has been described as a person who sets up his own business or industry through personal drive, initiative, skills and spirit of innovation aiming at high goals, (Drucker, 1985). The entrepreneur sees opportunities and identifies those which he translates his profits. The entrepreneur is quick to seize such opportunities for economic gain (Drucker, 1985). To be an entrepreneur requires that one be action oriented, highly motivated and a risk taker so as to achieve one's goals.

According to Drucker, entrepreneurship is the activity by an individual or group of individuals, who undertake to initiate, gain and maintain profit by production or distribution of goods and services. It is the process of providing a new product or service and intentional creation of value through organization by an individual contributor or small groups partners (Coulte, 2000). This Coulter process of creating something new and different by devoting the necessary time is accompanied by financial, psychological, and social risks. Once the process is successful, it is rewarded with monetary and personal satisfaction, (Gartner, 1990). There is no doubt therefore that an entrepreneur has a critical role in entrepreneurship and MSE activities.

It is argued that in Kenya the government has invested extensively towards implementing policies and programs specifically aimed at promoting the micro small enterprises sector (sessional paper No. 1986).

1.1 Definitions, Distinctions and Assumptions

Loucks (1988)[1] defines entrepreneurship as the pursuit of a discontinuous opportunity involving creation of an organization or sub-organization with intention to create value to participants

---

1   Kenneth Loucks (1988) Training Entrepreneurs for Small Business Creation: Lessons from Experience. ILO Publication No.26 – Geneve
ILO-International Labour Organization - Geneve
Peter Drucker (1985) Innovation and entrepreneurship: Practice and Principles (Butterworth – Heinemann, 1985)

The entrepreneur is the individual (or team) that identifies the opportunity, gathers the necessary resources, creates and is ultimately responsible for performance of the organization. In Loucks, strategies are designed to create jobs by assisting entrepreneurs to start and develop firms (Loucks, 1988. p.12)

Indeed entrepreneurship is the means whereby new organizations are formed with sole purpose of providing jobs and wealth creation, providing goods and services to the society as its critical components. This definition champions the behavioural aspect of entrepreneurship.

However, it is noted that growth, innovation and tenacity are common characteristics of entrepreneurship, to overcome difficulties. It is argued that they are merely consequences to the entrepreneurial behaviour. For example to survive, one needs a sanctuary where he can have reflection of the previous day's journey, renew their emotional resources and recalibrate their moral compass (Heifetz, Linsky 2002 p.65 – 74)[2]

1.2 What is Entrepreneurship?

Entrepreneurship is defined in two approaches, first entrepreneurship as related to the behaviour and an entrepreneur as a person who agitates in entrepreneurial activities.

In (Shapero1985) entrepreneurship is the process focusing on entrepreneurial support. This is confirmed by the enhanced interest in entrepreneurship which is apparent in significant growth in self- employment, company formation and great interest all over.[3]

It is also cited by Jean Baptise in the concept of combining factors of production. While (Schumpeter 1934) talked of an entrepreneur as carrying out new combinations hence known as "enterprise" which is driven by the entrepreneur. He contends the entrepreneur to be the one who carries new combinations and loss. He takes the responsibility of running it with other people. Schumpeter concludes that entrepreneurships are run by entrepreneurs. They are marshalling and committed to resources in the face of risk to pursue the opportunity that motivated a business idea (Baumol 1990, p.894 – 921)[4]

2   Ronald A. Heifetz and Marty Linsky. (2002). A Survival Guide for Leaders, Harvard Business Review, June 2002, p.65 – 74
3   Gartner B. WIliam. (1989). Who is an Entrepreneur? Is the Wrong Question. Entrepreneurship Theory and Practice Summer (1989), University of Baltimore, pp.47-68) U.S.A
4   William J.Baumol (1990),p. 894, Journal of Political Economy 1990, Vol. 98, no.5 pt 1, University of Chicago.

There are distinct features of entrepreneurs that Schumpeter has said about entrepreneurship. It involves creation of an organization to pursue a discontinuous opportunity, it is not limited to the pursuit of new ventures, entrepreneurship can also flourish in existing established organization and by acting a transition occurs at some point as change is eminent from these individual actions.

1.3 Who is an Entrepreneur?

It is a problem defining who an entrepreneur is and the question has remained a problem for most writers, scholars and researchers (Drucker, 1985).

There are a number of definitions by various authors which are empirically derived, for example Schumpeter, Schultz and McClelland (1961). This definition borders along economies and is psychological. William Gartner associates the entrepreneur with a set of activities involved in organization, creation, personal trait, and characteristics.

Literature appears to agree that there is no generic definition of an entrepreneur; if there is, it has not been discovered. Many researches in entrepreneurship have focused on the person of the entrepreneur. It is however questioned why certain individuals start firms when others with similar condition do not? For example, why did "Onome" start a venture? Because "Onome" has certain inner qualities. This question is used to answer the traits and differences that exist between entrepreneurs and non-entrepreneurs are an individual, "someone who initiates and actively operates the entrepreneurial venture."[5]

According to small business administration (SBA), successful entrepreneurs have, drive which is considered an important attribute. Entrepreneurs will stay for long hours and bear high stress and endless problems when they launch a new business (Dana, 1994).[6]
Examples of these challenges include loneliness time demands of the business, conflict from partners and employees and achievement needs. In the classical thinking of Richard Caultillion (1700), J.B Say (1815) Schumpeter (1949) and McClelland (1961), all conclude that an entrepreneur is one who is keen in leading the activities, is responsible for change of form and has genuine need for achievement.[7]

---

5 Leo Paul Dana (1994,p. 83 -102) International Note Coping with Entrepreneurial Stress: Evidence from Nigeria.
6 Leo Paul Dana (1994, p. 83-102) International Note coping with Entrepreneurial Stress: Evidence from Nigeria.
7 The concept of entrepreneurship becomes more clear due to scientist like McClelland (1969) who stressed need for achievement motive"

Schumpeter (1949) views entrepreneurs as those who bring resources together and combines them to generate profits. Vesper sees entrepreneurs as individuals driven by achievement orientation to seek challenges and new accomplishments.[8] Literature shows popular notions that most entrepreneurs are "born" with innate characteristics that propel them to create ventures (Holt, 2001, p.52).[9] It is evident that successful entrepreneurs are optimistic and have a keen sense of determination, enough amount of energy and a clear destiny.[10]

An entrepreneur is a risk taker; he/she is innovative. Those owners who are not innovative and are not growing their activities are not considered to be entrepreneurial. Indeed many researchers have experienced difficulty in determining the entrepreneurial behaviour as can be seen from the efforts of economists J.B Say (1815) and Schumpeter (1934) and psychologist McClelland (1961). The key components in their conclusions are management, administration, decision – making, risk taking, responsibility and innovation.

McClelland (1961) gives a psychological perspective of an entrepreneur as exercising some means of control over all the factors of production (land, labour, capital and organization) and process to ensure sufficiency for own consumption (household) and to sell for income generation.

However, it should be considered that a well defined entrepreneurial population does not exist in a particular sphere. But an attempt is made in this study to define the entrepreneur as a risk taker, innovative person who takes responsibility of creating a venture or business for purposes of generating income and seeks business growth and expansion as an avenue to increasing the profits. Hence micro and small enterprises that are not growth oriented and innovative are not entrepreneurial

This work adopted an operational definition of the entrepreneur as someone who initiates and actively operates the entrepreneurial venture/business (Coulter, 2000, p.25).

1.4 The Distinction Between an Entrepreneur and a Manager

It is important to note that there is a significant difference between a manger and an entrepreneur. Baumol (1961, p.64) defines a manager as an individual who oversees the day to day operations and efficiency

---

8   The entrepreneurs are people who work for themselves or for owners of the enterprise. The term is derived from the French word "entrependre" meaning to undertake. The entrepreneur undertakes to run an enterprise.

9   Karl Versper a researcher in entrepreneurship explains the nature and individual perception to endorse free enterprises."

10   Are entrepreneurs Born or made? "There is substantial evidence that entrepreneurial characteristics may be environmentally based"

of a continuous process. The task of a manager includes availing skilled manpower, machinery, and raw material, which are combined in proportions appropriate to produce outputs, minimize wastage, maximize resources, and execute contracts and marketing. In a nutshell, the manager discharges sound management in an organization to achieve the vision, mission, and objectives of the venture. The entrepreneur on the other hand, has the task of combining resources, locating new ideas and converting them into products and services. The entire organization must be lead by the entrepreneur.

Some writers agree with the Drucker's distinction by saying that the entrepreneur has the responsibility of establishing new products and new markets; he/she is different from an innovative manager whose duty is to ensure that operations are functioning effectively and efficiently. The entrepreneur must co-ordinate; direct others to direct the business to a new zone.[11]

The manager will supervise the productive activities, while the entrepreneur will plan, prepare and practice innovation and ultimately decide the destiny of the enterprise in pursuit of an opportunity. However, Coulter (2000) contends that an entrepreneur has clear intentions and therefore it is not accidental that they start a venture and engage in efforts to combine personal and contextual factors. In short, a manager does things right, while the entrepreneur does the right things. That is the thin line of distinction.

An entrepreneur (ahn'trapranur) is a person who organizes and manages a business undertaking, assuming the risk for the sake of profits. There is no age limit to start a business.

An entrepreneur must have communication skills, the ability to make oneself understood. To be successful, he/she must have the technical ability to understand his product and market. One should be able to consider the long and short term implications of decisions, his strengths and weaknesses, competition. He must have strategic management skills.

Early entrepreneurship programs were known as farming programs, productive enterprises or ownership. These were primarily involved in livestock and growing crops. Entrepreneurship today will involve planning, implementing and assuming financial risks, while keeping records to determine return on investments. Examples of micro and small enterprises are lawn maintenance, transport by *Boda boda*,[12]

---

11 The role and status of the entrepreneur. It is difficult to determine which status are entrepreneurial ones and which are not. (Coulter 2000 p.19)

12 'Boda boda' is an informal means of transport in the border towns of western Kenya by use of a bicycle

crop harvesting, fishing guide, tractor and farm equipment leasing, operating roadside fruit selling, making and selling Christmas and funeral wreaths and operating garage and engine repair. The micro and small business enterprises entrepreneur has to identify and recognize an opportunity and generate a business idea, product or service to address the opportunity.

Figure 1: Entrepreneurial Management Skills

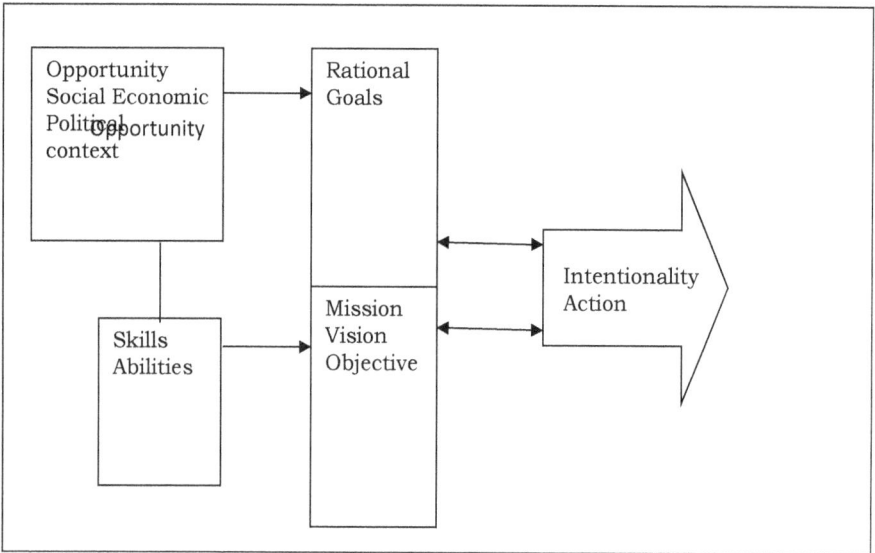

Source: Academy of Management Review

The role of the entrepreneur has evolved with time and professional entrepreneurs rely more on intellect and / or guts instincts (Lee, 2000, Venkataraman, 2000). Richman compares entrepreneurs over time. The old entrepreneur was a boss while the modern one is a leader. Then, they were selective: today they are open. Many were self reliant, now they are inquisitive, they are net workers. Where once they took quick decisions, now they take time to build consensus. For the purposes[13] of the work, a manager is defined as an "individual who does not own the venture whereas an entrepreneur is the individual who owns the business or the owner and manager of the venture who maximizes opportunities.

---

13   Drucker says that entrepreneurship does not just happen out of blue but arises in response to what the entrepreneur sees as an untapped and undeveloped opportunities (Coulter 2000p.8).

Joo-Heon le, S.Venkataraman (2000), p. 1-41, Aspiration level, labour market evaluation, and the decision to become an entrepreneur. The Darden school of Business Administration University of Virginia lee @darden Virginia.edu

1.5 Micro and Small Enterprises (MSEs)

Micro and small enterprises are a response to the needs of the community and society in terms of activities, goods and services. MSEs cover a range of sectors differently while addressing market opportunities. This diversity makes it difficult to categorise or immediately compare their performances sector–wise or even enterprise-wise. Indeed, to analyse the problem of MSEs in Kenya is made more complicated by the irregular and unofficial terms used to describe them.[14] The ambiguous names and terminologies utilized makes MSEs united in diversity. For example, the term *Jua Kali* does not necessarily mean *"out in the sun.'* A doctor's clinic will be referred to as *"Jua Kali"* although it will be housed in a decent modern building. The use of the term *"jua kali"* simply implies the size of the enterprise.   Equally, a *"matatu"* operator will refer to her business as *Jua Kali* to mean that it is a micro and small enterprise (MSE). A computer workshop, property manager or legal firm could be comfortable to introduce themselves as micro and small enterprises.

The definition by many authors regarding MSEs tends towards addressing statutory regulatory measures, statistical records and numbers or volumes of employees or sales turnover and amount of capital invested. particular definitions are used to express classification of MSEs for establishing eligibility for government or donors and are based on the functional characteristics, for example management,   services,goods,ownership,gender,   specialization, technique and market orientation, all of which are used to determine performance. Presently, attempts have been made to explicitly define micro and small enterprises in Kenya in the manner outlined below.[15] Employment does not necessarily mean salaries and wages. It simply means being engaged in the activities of MSEs in Kenya consisting of business or activities of self-employed artisan's i.e. Jua Kali enterprises with one or two employees. Some have few employees-cottage industries, solo entrepreneurs, small enterprises in both the informal and formal sectors employing 1 to 10 or more employees conducting business, in manufacturing, supplies, trade, distribution, service, transport,construc tion,assembly,repair and maintenance. The MSE(s) may also be engaged in professional activities like chemistry, Accountancy, Consultancy Agency services, legal practice, Medical, survey etc. (baseline survey 1999, p.12).

14   Kenneth King and Simon McGrath, 1999.p. 144 -223.

15   "The term micro and small enterprises therefore covers a range of establishments, including informal sector employing up to 50 persons (National Micro and small Enterprises Baseline Survey 1999,p.12).

Using the size criterion, Mc McCormick (1993) Categorizes Kenyan MSEs into four. Micro business will employ six or fewer employees, small enterprises have 7 to 10 workers, medium size firms have 11 to 50 workers and large enterprises will employ over 50 workers.[16] Kenya like the rest of the developing world faces the challenge of providing gainful employment to its employable population. Most employment is sought in urban areas. This puts immense pressure on the available resource in a largely agricultural economy. This is what has come to ignite what is known as the informal and formal sector, micro and small enterprises (McCormick, 1998), hence giving MSEs an important position in the formulation of policy.

An empirical study of Kenya and Bangladesh shows increasingly high incidence of under and unemployment, prompting citizens to resort to self-employment in micro and small enterprises (Bulletoft, 1996). Poverty has grown to such high levels that even donor efforts have had less impact than expected. The quest for industrialized country status has stalled in the formative stages because vital resources were not established.

Rasmussen (1992) argues that by treating petty producers as marginal to the mainstream economy, governments have ignored a significant contribution to employment, new products and markets. It is acknowledged today in developing countries that MSEs are a great source of employment creation.

The phenomenon of micro and small enterprises are not uniform. These activities were referred to as informal sector in 1980s because of their unique composition and heterogeneity. The description of MSE activities is small, produced at home, in the street, or in designed industrial settings. For example in Kenya such settings are Gikomba, Kenyatta market, Kariobangi light industries, Ruaraka's industrial area, and EPZ at Athi River. The major activities are metal-based workshops, garment-makers, printing, and fabrications. Micro and small enterprise activities are a source of innovation and creativity and a sponge to absorb the unemployed (Audretsch, 2002).

It is argued that micro and small enterprise activities has increased in recent times, providing entrepreneurs with tremendous ability in adapting to change in market conditions and spotting profitable opportunities. The changes that have occurred in Kenya range from structural adjustments, a measure which includes privatization, deregulation, removing import restrictions and price controls (Mc McCormick, 1996).

---

16   McCormick .D. (1998). Gender in small Enterprises Development in Kenya: An Institutional Analysis, IDS, University of Nairobi –Kenya.

However some of these measures have also worked negatively for micro and small enterprises entrepreneurs by striking them out of highly competitive activities, which could give them quick returns on investment (King and Mc Grath, 1999).From studies of small business in Europe, it is suggested that such firms have the capacity to overcome and achieve efficiency, similar to that of large firms. However, this success is   attributed to factors like tradition of self employment, extensive entrepreneurial net-workers, division of labour characterized by innovation and efficiency (for example industrial patents) and institutional, political and environmental support for promotion of coexistence of competition and joint venture cooperation.

1.6 Distinctions Between a Study of Behaviour of an Entrepreneur and Entrepreneurial Behaviour

According to Wickham (1998)[17], the entrepreneur plays a critical role in shaping and maintaining the economy by creating new value. It is recognized that primarily a combination of factors of production bring forth value that satisfies human needs. The entrepreneur, using individuals working together in completing certain tasks, brings together the factors of production. The coordination of these tasks is known as organization, hence referred to as the fourth factor of production.

The entrepreneur ensures that competition is controlled between different suppliers and that people can gain by maximization and by providing efficiency. The entrepreneurs look out for excess profits and are willing to take and accept lower profits or what they perceive to be near a true market rate.[18] The entrepreneur accepts risk on behalf of others, something that many people will generally want to avoid. The chance that something will go wrong no matter how well we plan is what is known as risk, and when we do not know what the future will bring, the lack of knowledge is the situation we refer to as uncertainty. The entrepreneur comes in handy to remove the risk off people's hands. Status of an entrepreneur will refer to that position in a community and role to the behaviour required by definition and of an occupant (McClelland, 1961). Research shows that the occupants of a given position or status will not behave according to the role requirements of the position (Mc Cleland, 1961)[19].

17 "Some economists regard entrepreneurship as a kind of factor which acts on the other three to combine in productive ways" (Wickham 1998 p. 10)
18   Dorothy   McCormick.   (1996).The   Impact   of   Economic   Reform   on Entrepreneurial Activity: A Theoretical Framework for Analysing Small Enterprises. The Independent Review 1996. Institute of Development Studies (UoN).
19 Mc Clelland (1961).The Achieving Society, London: Collier- McMillan Ltd.

However it is important to note that there are entrepreneurs who are "growth oriented" and will pursue opportunities to maximize the potential of their venture; independent entrepreneurs will aim at working for themselves. Entrepreneurs as those occupying entrepreneurial status need not show entrepreneurs who are "growth oriented" and will pursue opportunities to maximize the potential of their venture; independent entrepreneurs will aim at working for themselves.[20]

Entrepreneurs as those occupying entrepreneurial status need not show entrepreneurial behaviour. Other people in society may display components of entrepreneurial role behaviour even if they are not necessarily occupying the status of an entrepreneur. In this book, the primary focus is on entrepreneurial role behaviour as opposed to the behaviours of an entrepreneur.

The personality of an entrepreneur is an important theme in this work. The entrepreneur is definitely inspiring because he is a motivating role model. For example, if an entrepreneur achieves success, they are regarded as great; but if they fail, then they are not (wickham, 1998).

Research has shown that an entrepreneur is driven to create his own situation, which in turn is the motivating factor to innovate and create a new institution. it is evident that some managers working as professionals leave and start their own ventures to make up for their inability to fit into established firms.

In the influential study by David McClelland in the sixties, the need for achievement was a fundamental driving force in the personality of successful entrepreneurs. It is suggested, therefore, that entrepreneurial behaviour is determined by genetic complement i.e. by nature and earlier experiences in life where talents are nurtured and in extreme conditions by a combination of both traits.[21] However, these interactions are critical and controversial in society.

We are saying that behaviour develops continuously and interacts in a setting (social) rather than in an individual. From the foregoing, it can be said that entrepreneurial behaviour is a social phenomenon. The entrepreneurs are predisposed by their experience. In this view, we can conclude that "entrepreneurs are not born, they are made."[22]

---

20   Philip A.Wickham.(1998).strategic Entrepreneurship: A Decision Making Approach to New Venture Creation and Management. Pitman Publishing.

21   The Achieving Society, London: Collier-McMillan ltd.

22   " A person is not once and for all entrepreneurial" (Wickham, 1998, p.15), Strategic Entrepreneurship, Great Britain, Redwood Books.

Figure 2: The entrepreneurial process – Focus, Fit and Configuration

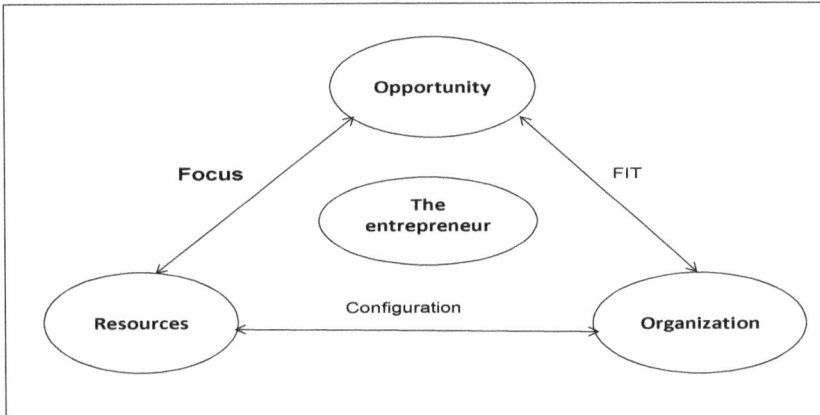

Source: *Philip Wick ham.(1998) . Strategic Entrepreneurship: A Decision Making Approach to New Venture Creation and Management, p.31.*

1.7 Family Micro and Small Enterprises

It is important to define the family firm for purposes of replication or for determining characteristics of the population. In a family business, control is held by an individual or family and managed by a family member.

Transfer of such firm or business is to a subsequent generation. Various studies conducted on family firms reveal that they have a multi-generational dimension. This distinguishes family entrepreneurship from all other type of entrepreneurial behaviour. Family MSE(s) contribute a great deal to G.N.P. and wages and they are normally small in size. In the USA, one third of the fortune 500 is family firms.

Further, research has also indicated that a large proportion of sole proprietorships are family micro and small enterprises. In the USA, 75-90% of all firms are often counted as family owned and operated. Several authors have indicated that in developed countries, for example USA, large corporations hired close relatives or in-laws to hold management positions. Fortune 500 shows evidence of family occupying a significant proportion of decision-making positions in micro and small enterprises.

In a survey of the fortune 500, a staggering 175 MSE(s) were found to be family managed, whereas 150 out of Fortune 500 were controlled and owned by an individual or family of a single family. Indeed, the true position of family controlled MSEs is not clearly known as no study to replicate Fortune work has ever been undertaken in this part of the world, that is Kenya and sub-Saharan region.

While it is argued that entrepreneurship is not restricted to a single act but is instead a label to a multidisciplinary field, it is also believed that in entrepreneurship, family businesses are speculating.

However, a nation-wide survey (Kenya) indicated that family micro and small enterprises encounter numerous obstacles. Only about 25% have a written succession plan. In another random sample, it was found that 42% of the firms had a written business plan; only 21% had a succession plan. Our research found a positive correlation between strategic planning and continuity planning. It also revealed that founder members resisted succession planning. This was confirmed as a common phenomenon in family MSEs.

From casual observations of family MSEs, the factor of resistance is manifested and prevalent in local enterprises, especially the Asian dominated family MSEs.It is not without conflict of interest, sometimes resulting in prolonged litigations. However the factors that influence resistance are multilevel and include individual, organizational, family and environmental, hence "succession conspiracy" which explains why the stakeholders, who are family advisors and a non-family manager, conspire in the resistance. It is empirically proven that the problem of succession is more critical to the original entrepreneur because he will hang on to watch while the heirs feel overshadowed and frustrated, constraining the entrepreneurial ability to grow the firm to greater heights.

Beyond the usual obstacles to communicate, family emotions tend to complicate the understanding of the situation. Management of the company is wrapped up in one person: the founder. There is pronounced gap between the owner and the manager. Below is an example of a model of family business.

Figure 3: Life Cycle of the family Business.

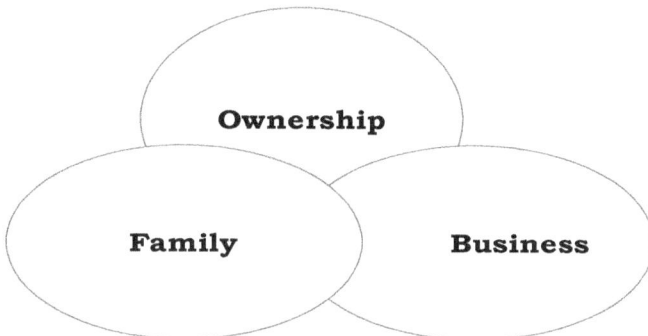

The three-circle model represents the behaviour of a family business. It is easier to understand the sources of conflict and priorities in the family owned enterprises (Krister Ahlstro'm, 1998)[23].

Figure 4: Governance Structure in Three – Circle Model

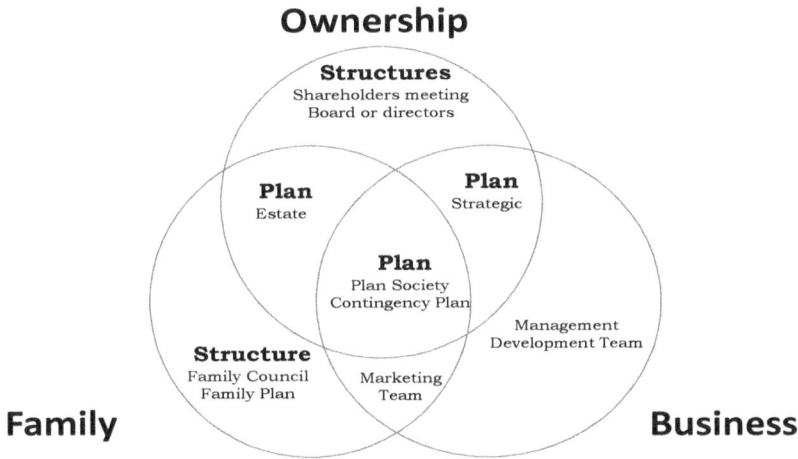

Ownership

Structures
Shareholders meeting
Board or directors

Plan
Estate

Plan
Strategic

Plan
Plan Society
Contingency Plan

Structure
Family Council
Family Plan

Marketing
Team

Management
Development Team

Family

Business

Source: Kielin E.Gersick, John A. Davis, Marion McCollon Hampton. (1997). Life Circles of the Family business, Harvard Business School Press, Boston Massachusetts, p. 226

1.8 Sole Entrepreneur

In this form of business, the owner controls and maintains sole and complete responsibility over the venture (coulter, 2000).It is simple because there are no legal requirements for establishing the entity. In Kenya, one needs to obtain necessary local business permits and licenses to operate and registration for personal identification number (PIN) AND Value Added Tax (VAT). The sole entrepreneurs run their businesses in the simplest freedom as they please. There are disadvantages with Sole Entrepreneurs in terms of unlimited liabilities. For example, the debt incurred by business has the potential of making the owner to lose all that they invested and much more. Personal assets such as house or car can be sold to liquidate such debts.

In the UK, a large number of MSEs who practiced solo had a high incidence of failure due to poor financial control (barrow, 1995).They did not have a business plan that was beyond twelve months of business trading and lacked visionary planning which severely restricted their access to financial support from banks, hence contributing to financial

---

23   Krister Ahlstro'm. (1998.Governing the Family-owned Enterprise, Harvard Business Review (January – Feb 1998,p. 115 -123).

failure and lack of control. Mike Davis, Managing Director of MSE banking, Barclays Bank PLC, advises that owners should plan and forecast. In new business, the first year is critical for determining success or failure because of lack of achieving first year targets.

1.9 Partnership

In partnership, two or more business owners share the management and risk of the business. Partnerships have numerous problems no matter who are involved, whether the partners are family members or good friends (counter, 2000). Coulter recommends a written agreement by legal counsel. Each partner should ensure compliance with all the agreements in the partnership deed.

However, taxes and liabilities are passed on to the partners, since they are exposed to unlimited personal liabilities. The partnership enjoys a variety of resources, for example finances and pool of talents that are unavailable to one person who is on his/her own. It is important to mention that authority should be divided between partners to avoid (unilateral) decisions that can lead to conflicts.

2.0 Barriers Encountered By MSEs

The national MSE baseline survey (Aleke, Maku, Oyombe & Charms, 1999) reported that MSEs faced severe constraints in accessing essential facilities to run their business. The report cited competition and lack of markets to be problem number one to most entrepreneurs. It mentioned a whole host of problems like lack of credit, poor roads and transport network, raw materials shortages, dishonest workers, and lack of electricity, among others.

In the UK economy, MSEs play a great role, accounting for 99% of all business in the country. It is a source of new employment and jobs. The enterprise is responsible for 46% of the workforce (barrow, 1995). Barrow notes that by 1996, there were an estimated 3.7 billion active business in UK; of these 2.5 billion are made up of solo traders or partners without employees, while 58% of the solo entrepreneurs are registered for VAT, showing an increase in turnover and performance.

According to Rigby and Zook (2002), a company can fail to achieve its objectives if they do not apply the lessons of free trade to the market for new ideas by reaching out and considering the competitive risks. Rigby and Zook[24] contend that companies that collaborate with others, for example on their research and development, end up reaping higher percentages of their total sales from new products than those that do not collaborate at all.

24   Darrell Rigby and Chris Zook. (2002). Open-Market Innovation, Harvard Business Review, October 2002, p.81 – 85.

2.1 Legal and Regulatory Frameworks

The legal, regulatory and tax frameworks affect the dynamics of enterprise growth and by extension the micro and small enterprises (Mead, 1993) a conference held in Abidjan, Nigeria in 1993 proposed that a good policy towards development and implementation of small enterprises is necessary as an agent of change.

There are three dimensions towards MSEs that are constrained by legal and regulatory frameworks. These are birth, survival and growth. Such constraints are manifested in, for example, the effect of compliance, cost and the tax framework on the dynamics of entrepreneurship. Many MSEs do not last long and the attrition rate is sustained (Eakin, 2000).[25] The rate of job creation through start-ups among MSEs is inversely related to rising police sweeps in "wrong places" which is a common problem in many developing countries. A recent example is from Zimbabwe, where government forces destroyed MSEs (BBC Media, June 2005).This genuine desire by policy makers to keep order-but which ends up in the destruction of small enterprises- is also seen in the central business district (CBD)in Nairobi. However, it is difficult to achieve neat conditions. It is impossible. Some argue that such efforts are meant to protect formal businesses, deemed to have permanent licensed premises, from competition.

The Kenyan MSE experience attributes closure of business to legal regulatory or fiscal problems. The government regulates and controls economic activities leaving no room for MSEs to flourish and innovate. Mead (1993) cites bulldozing and harassment as common headaches to MSEs.[26] These contribute to direct firm losure while in several other countries, for example Botswana and Malawi, firms close due to shortage of capital. Government policies made it difficult for MSEs to obtain funds.[27] Mead adds that it takes two months to obtain a license and to meet all obligations required to be compliant.

In many countries, taxes were reported as a serious problem for most start-ups. For example, in mid 1980s in South Africa, many types of businesses were deemed illegal and thus extremely restricted (mead,1993).This confirmed entrepreneurial activity to particular places. In Nairobi's CBD, Police and City Council terms occasionally sweep the

25 Douglas Holtz Eakin. (2000). Public policy towards Entrepreneurship, Small Business Economics 15, 283- 291. Netherlands.

26 Donald Mead. (1993). The Way in which the legal regulatory and tax framework affects the Dynamics of Enterprise Growth. Department of Economics, Michigan State University (U.S.A), SME Conference-PME Abidjan, 30 Nov- 2nd Dec, 1993.

27 Rosalind Levacic. 1987). Economic Policy- Making, New jersey: Wheat sheaf Books, Sussex Barnes & Noble Books.

"wrong"places i.e. Hawkers in the name of keeping order. Malawi had 10% closures due to shortage of raw material, restriction in importation laws, duty and tariff.

It has been shown that there is a higher MSEs start up rate if legal and regulatory constraints are eased. Evidence from research indicates that in Kenya, MSEs attribute closure to legal, regulatory or fiscal problems. The component of taxation has impacted negatively on MSEs. It is suspected that a one-stop shop approach to taxes will precipitate growth, with a simplified taxation regime for MSEs and a single interface between central government and local government. An example would be one permit to conduct business within Kenya boundaries. This will replace the many cumbersome taxes for MSEs.

Casual observation in Kenya reveals that MSEs as a segment in the economy are ignored by commercial banks. The banks prefer "niche" segments. It is only MFI and SACCOs that sometimes cover MSE(s). Evidence from the cited studies shows that there is a direct effect of compliance cost that firms. Many failed entrepreneurs cited legal regulatory or tax issues as principal causes for going out of business. In-directly the legal and regulatory framework contributes to firm closure through lack of access to credit, raw materials, intermediate inputs and operating capital.

The sessional Paper no.3 of 2004 cites the Major shortcomings to the MSE sector development as inappropriate policy design and weak implementation systems that do not support effective monitoring, leading to failure in addressing the specific needs of micro and small entrepreneurs. It is evident that some laws are hindrances to MSEs. Some of these are cumbersome, for instance local authority by-law s and lengths processes of dealing with government agencies. These affect MSEs by diverting their hard earned resources from wealth creation to housekeeping.

Accordingly, centralization of certain services also pose a problem to MSEs, for example the registration of business names, licensing, judicial systems which are complex and expensive, insecurity of property and tenure (Sessional Paper No. 3, 2004)[28]. Taxation is a problem for micro and small enterprises. According to a survey conducted by Marrison, Lecomte & Oudin (1994), compliance with tax obligations constrained MSEs through inspection and sanction. We know that indirect taxes, which are favoured by many governments, have great impact on any single activity of the micro and small enterprises.

---

28 GOK (2004) Sessional Paper No. 3 of 2004 on Development of Micro and Small Enterprises for Wealth Creation and Employment Generation.

For example, MSEs have no mechanism of passing the tax on so as to take full advantage of tax procedures.

MSEs are not opposed to taxation in principle; all they require is commensurate public service such as access to water and electricity. Alternatively, it would be better for MSEs if such taxes or charges accorded them certain rights when procuring services and goods (Marrison, Lecomte, Oudin, 1994).[29] There is a huge unfavourable taxation regime. An example is VAT which is affecting both goods and services and at all levels of consumption. It increases transaction and administration costs and inhibits cash flow when the agents appointed by the tax administration withhold the money. We cite withholding Tax and withholding VAT as some of the taxes that pose difficulty to the entrepreneur. Sometimes, refunds on excess taxes delay inordinately, posing a critical problem to micro and small enterprises.

2.2 Entrepreneurial Behaviour

Risk taking is at the centre of entrepreneurial behaviour. The attributes coming out of research were that sales were done at above competition prices, trading on credit was to know and identified customers and partnership activities were conducted to pull scarce resources together (Schumpeter, 1934).

Research has shown a huge body of entrepreneurs who may have personality traits that are different from those of others in the population. This results in a belief that entrepreneurial behaviour. For example , McClelland's research has characterized entrepreneurs with a high need for achievement.[30] According to Ulrich and Cole (1981)[31] these individuals tend to operate on set goals, achieve these goals in their own effort, solve problems and require feedback on accomplished tasks. The entrepreneurs will have internal focus of control and believe in determining their own fate within a set limit.

Schere (1982)[32] observes that entrepreneurs have high tolerance than others for ambiguity and novelty. These characteristics may underlie

29   Christian Marrison, Henri-Bernard Solignac Lecomte, Xavier Oudin. (1994). Micro Enterprises and the Institutional Framework in developing Countries. OECD publication, Paris cedex 16. France.

30   D.C McClelland, The Achieving Society.(1961). Journal of Personality and Social Psychology, April 1965, p.389 -392.

31   Ulrich Thomas A. and George Cole, Journal of Business Management, October 1987, p.33 - 39.

32   David N. Allan and Syender Rehman. Small Business Incubators: A Positive Environment for Entrepreneurship, Journal of Small Business Management (July 1985, p.13 -21).

the entrepreneurs' impetus to innovate. Ulrich and Cole add that other traits associated to entrepreneurs are autonomy, independence and dominance.

Figure 5: Entrepreneurial Learning Style

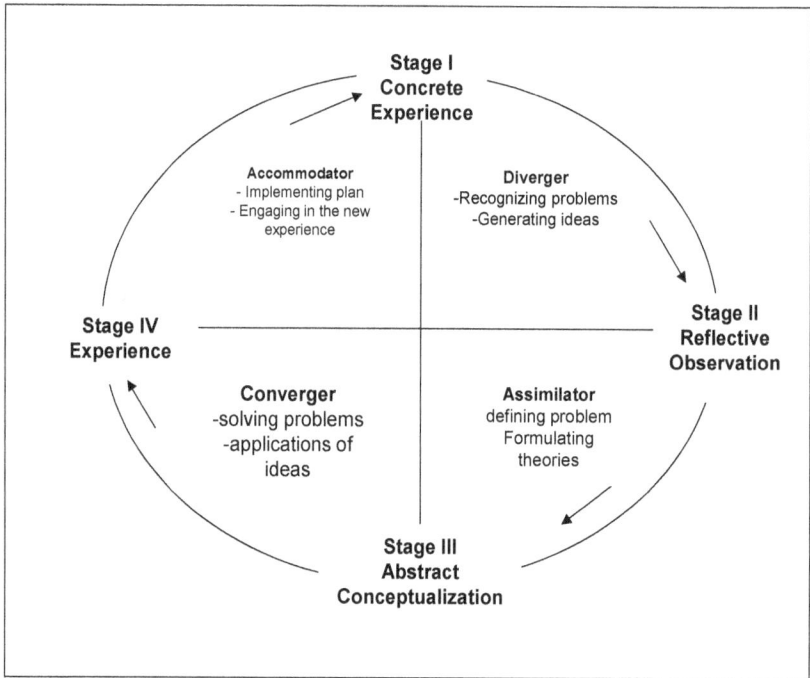

Adopted from Journal of Small Business Management (October 1987, p. 34)

"The four pedagogical categories are defined by the changes they are best at facilitating in human behaviour."

We in Kenya are criticised for low entrepreneurial activity. The government has not done enough in creating small business incubators. These are supposed to be facilities that provide enabling climate at earlier stages of growth of companies, by availing rental space, shared office, services, and business consultancy services.

Allan and Rehman (1985) recognise that few businesses make it through their earlier years. Among the reasons they cite for business failure are management problems, lack of capital, lack of knowledge of market niches, since their intention is often to exploit virgin market segments.

Awareness of the significant social and economic roles contributed by micro and small enterprises and the importance of entrepreneurship to the growth of the economy cannot be under estimated (Loucks, 1988). Indeed, this is true of both developed and developing economies of the world.[33] According to Loucks, the developed economies have benefited from MSEs by way of new jobs created over the last decade and the innovation and invention that pioneered the creation of industries. Examples are microelectronics, information technology and biochemistry. whereas the developing economies have experienced capital shortage and growing labour surplus, they have not been left behind in enjoying the benefits of job creation, markets, incubator for entrepreneurial talents and testing ground for new products and industries. Additional, MSEs enhance and promote a safe environment than do large industries. They also stimulate personal saving and improve rural welfare.

In summary, the behaviour of the entrepreneur is characterized by risk taking, innovativeness and the knowledge of desired results and individual responsibilities of the entrepreneur.

2.3 Innovativeness

Innovativeness refers to newness. Innovation is a specific function of entrepreneurship, be it in a business, government service, institution or a new business enterprise started by one individual or a family.

Druckers argues that most innovative business ideas come from methodical analysis, which lies either in an industry, social or demographic trends (Coulter, 2002).Entrepreneurs have in common a certain kind of personal commitment to systematic practices of innovation. It can be confidently said that entrepreneurial roles involve by definition, using a new method and better ways. Innovation requires that the entrepreneur discovers, searches new areas in knowledge, information on markets, techniques, goods and services. The new ideas have to be translated into products. Writing on innovation, Levitt[34] (2002) notes that ideas are useless unless used. The proof of their value is their implementation. Zook (2002) contends that the entrepreneur must reach out for new ideas in an open market.[35] Pearson (2002) looks at innovation as a process of beginning with the right mind set, unsettling the organization, being hard-headed about strategy because good ideas often flow from the process of taking a hard look at customers, competitors and the business all at once.[36]

---

33   Kenneth Loucks. (1988). ILO Training entrepreneurs for small business creation lessons from experience, management series No.26. International Labour Office, Geneva.

34   Theodore Levitt, Creativity is not enough: The Innovative Enterprise. Harvard Business Review, August 2002,p. 137 – 145.

35   Darrell Rigby and Chris Zook, Open Market Innovation, Harvard Business Review, (October 2002, p.137 – 145).

36   Audrall E.Pearson, Tough Minded Ways to get Innovative: The Innovative Enterprises, Harvard Business Review, Aug.202, p.117-124

2.4 Individual Responsibility

It is argued that the entrepreneurial role is squarely assumed. The implication of this is that it is an individual and personal responsibility. According to McClelland (1961), the entrepreneur has the final and ultimate responsibility to take decisions affecting the venture.Kirzner (1982) contends that entrepreneurs assume the financial risk and responsibility for management of firms at the start-up phase with attributes of entrepreneurial conviction to understand and take moderate risks, set moderate achievement goals and completing a task that involves something unique. Schumpeter has described the entrepreneurial responsibility from the perspective of economic contribution whereby the entrepreneur is an innovator, taking the central role of generating a new idea as a sole and personal commitment. In the words of Kirzner (p.273), these individuals called entrepreneurs are individuals who search for and identify profit opportunities.[37] Indeed the decisions made by the entrepreneur are complex and affect the life of the business from all levels. Such responsibilities are individualistic. The entrepreneur has to accept blame and praise, failure and success.

The foregoing discussion leads us to ask: what factors account for entrepreneurial role and behaviour? No study has focused on matching entrepreneurial role behaviour and factors that influence the same. Existing studies relate the performance of an entrepreneur with certain factors that are then assumed to underlie entrepreneurial role behaviour. However, an article by Hirsch and Brush (1986) noted that entrepreneurs who were successful in new ventures had the advantage of having experienced dealing with money and performing financial responsibilities, and had achievement, opportunity and job satisfaction as strongest motivators for starting a successful venture.

2.5. Factors that Determine Entrepreneurial Behaviour

These are innovativeness, alertness to opportunity, uncertainty, responsibility, education, access to credit, experience, culture, environment, gender and infrastructure.

2.5.1 Innovativeness

Writing on the relationship between the dynamics of technology and business enterprises, Schumpeter (1985) suggests that innovativeness

---

37 "The entrepreneurial function is to notice what people have overlooked" Kirzner, "The Theory of entrepreneurship in Economic Growth,"1982, p.273.

is inherent in entrepreneurship. The entrepreneurs think of how to come up with a new product and the channels of introducing the new products to the market. Innovation involves change, revolutionizing, transforming and introducing new approaches (Coulter, 2000).

In their endeavour to renovate, entrepreneurs take care of customer's needs by creating new products. In the USA, entrepreneurs are respected since they serve as a "bridge" to development and innovations Schumpeter (1934) believed that with the process of creative destruction of old, inefficient and ineffective approaches, inferior products are replaced with better ones which gave rise to innovativeness in entrepreneurship. Schumpeter contends that entrepreneurial ventures were a driving force in innovation.

The CEOs of such giants as IBM, AT&T, Genentech, Mercle, and Pilkington included technical experts in their highest decision circles. Quinn (1985) notes that Genentech had its original plan expressed as a vision: "We expect to be the first company to commercialize the DNA technology and we need to build a major profitable corporation to manufacture and market products to benefit mankind." Such visions attract quality people to the company and give focus to their creative and entrepreneurial drives.

2.5.2 Alertness to Opportunity

According to Drucker (1985), entrepreneurs involve themselves in maximizing opportunities. He says that entrepreneurship does not just take place out of the blues; it is generated as a result of a response to what the entrepreneur sees as undeveloped and untapped opportunities. In other words, it is to perceive opportunities that would sufficiently enhance innovations (Coulter, 2000).

2.5.3 Uncertainty

According to Knight, uncertainty confuses many economists. Knight contends that enterprise does not collect windfalls and bear losses that are unanticipated. Entrepreneurs contribute to the performance of useful functions.

Entrepreneurial behaviour is more useful to parts of economics as entrepreneurs are associated with equilibrium. If they are not disturbed by changes, entrepreneurial abilities will add to economic value. For example, the interval between the time of production and the sale of output is a source of risk and uncertainty.

2.5.4 Responsibility

The role of the entrepreneur has been assumed to mean taking personal responsibilities for actions taken (McClelland, 1961; Drucker, 1985; Coulter, 2000).The entrepreneur has to work to remove impediments or reduce them, create a good attitude and provide for proper tools and habitable structures. The entrepreneur has to focus on relationships that are centered on entrepreneurship, making sure that workers have incentives, rewards, and compensation. The right decisions have to be made and responsibility for them be assumed by the entrepreneur. It does not matter what the outcome will be; all consequences must be accepted (Drucker, 1985).

Figure 6: Entrepreneurial Strategy

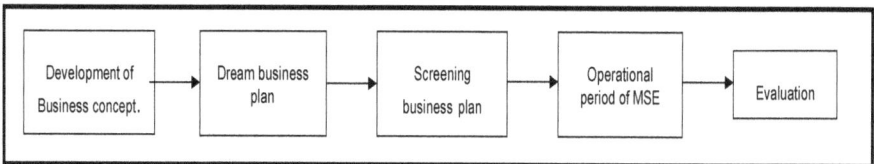

Research underscores the centrality of a business plan in a start-up business. The plan addresses the type of activities, target groups and strategy, market analysis that outlines the competition, allocation of different and critical tasks and financial provisions (Gartner, 1985). A business plan helps the entrepreneur to detail every simple aspect of their micro and small enterprises in a more coherent strategy.

2.5.5 Education

Education contributes a lot to managerial skills, technical abilities and techniques needed to undertake risk. Educated entrepreneurs have a broad perception of risk and innovation. Their analytical power is enhanced and they are better prepared for the challenges a head.

Schultz (1980) argues that the acquired abilities, enhanced by education and training, contribute to the crop land can be by irrigation, drainage and application of fertilizers. On the other hand, the productive capacity of high Yielding new varieties, of wheat exceeds the traditional varieties."We are saying here that educational capacity as a factor can determine entrepreneurial activities, hence behaviour. In modern parlance, we talk of capacity building, meaning education, training and development.

Education as a tool in the hands of entrepreneurs provides creative ability. Many writers in entrepreneurship have cited the education component as a strong influence on entrepreneurial behaviour. It increases analytical power, mathematical/arithmetic abilities and independent decision-making.

Training is a process of affecting change in behaviour. Bwisa (2000) sees education as a supply of specific skills, knowledge or attitudes required to meet a certain purpose. Education determines entrepreneurial capacities in estimating risks. For example, the doctor relies on the X-ray report to make diagnostic conclusions. Similarly, the accountant uses the "balance sheet to determine the performance of the organization," (Maragia, 1990, p.3)[38].

2.5.6 Access to Credit

A report by the Government of Kenya (sessional paper No.2 of 1999) noted that entrepreneurs with access to credit or financial assistance are likely to perform well in their venture than those who lack such support. For the entrepreneurs to expand their operation, it is imperative that funds are available.

A large proportion of entrepreneurs in Africa are obstructed by lack of funding capital. This hinders industrial development's(S) are hampered by lack of access to credit. This forms a major constraint to growth. The more affected are female entrepreneurs because they lack tangible security since they cannot inherit land and buildings which are commonly used as collateral.

Where the credit is available, it is often unaffordable to the informal sector MSEs. This is in addition to the banks viewing this sector as having high risk in recovery of credit (sessional paper no.3, 2004).

2.5.7 Access to Credit in Kenya

Lack of access to credit inhibits the growth of the MSE Sector. Women entrepreneurs are particularly disadvantaged since they lack tangible collateral (security).traditionally, lenders will ask for the title deed and not innovative strategies for leading. This affects entrepreneurial behaviour.

As said previously, the formal financial system in Kenya (banks) view MSEs as potential risk areas that are not commercially attractive for their money. This makes it difficult for entrepreneurs to procure or get access to credit. The problem is more critical to MSEs in rural areas. This factor contributes to the slow pace of MSEs graduating from informal to

---

38 Isaac Maragia. (1990).The Accounting profession: power and politics in organization Context. Prepared for the doctorate course, management and financial control-concepts and methods for archaeology of Accounting (5p), University of Lund, Spring 1990.

formal status. Access to finance, skills shortage and market linkages are key impediments in this regard.

2.5.8 Motivation

McClelland emphasizes the need for achievement in the entrepreneur. The entrepreneur has an urge to create, to build something and not to live like other people around him. This achievement singles out the entrepreneur from the rest of society. Microsoft's Bill Gates is an outstanding example in the word of information communication technology (ICT).

The achievement motive propels the entrepreneur to diversify, expand and innovate while thinking of new markets, more products and greater populations of customers. The innovative entrepreneur strives for higher levels of excellence. McClelland contends that motivation is "a process of providing for action" (1961, p. 26). This behaviour springs forth from individual needs as internal stimuli compelling actions.

Motivation is a directed or exerted effort towards some reward,gain,profit, and payoff: It is evident that an entrepreneur who is motivated goes out of his/her way to do something he/she could not do if not motivate enough. Such entrepreneurs exhibit personal responsibility and seek realistic risks, whereby the desire for feedback is guaranteed.

Studies conducted in Kenya have revealed that men and women like to be in business because of the need to be independent. Futher, the studies confirmed that even those with stable jobs and who are comparatively well paid were quitting to start their own ventures.

Drucker (1985) argues that motivated entrepreneurs are imaginative, disciplined and innovative, and are accountable to the business.

For McClelland (1960), "need achievement" is a social factor that characterizes successful entrepreneurs. Such entrepreneurs see far and wide as the risk factor stimulates them to greater efforts.

An entrepreneurial idea does not come out of the blues. People have ideas for new combinations of resources and are predisposed to think along some lines because something has sparked the idea. McClelland's (1996) work identified risk taking, need for achievement and need for control as "typical" entrepreneurial characteristics. Casson (1982) and legendary jack Brash epitomize these qualities. Empirical research has revealed that young people dominate in the possession of business ideas (Scott and Twoney, 1988). Drucker (1985), Scott, Kirzner (1979; 1985) call the perceived opportunity for profits the trigger factor, the impetus for entrepreneurial activity.

In the supply of the entrepreneurial events, constraining factors are those that discourage entrepreneurial activities and reduce the quantity and quality of innovative ideas, for example legal systems, markets, information and excessive regulation. Baumol (1990) underscores the importance of directional factors that shape both the entrepreneurial ideas and the means used to implement them. such factors influence entrepreneurs to undertake one activity rather than another, pushing the exercise of entrepreneurship in a particular direction.[39]

Kinyanjui et al. (1997) who have taken the position of Schum Peters, stress entrepreneurship and contends that it is necessary to establish a relationship between the motivation and firm performance and the "pull" factors of market opportunities rather than the "push' factors considered to be negative.[40]

2.5.9 Experience

Entrepreneurs with know-how and experience are likely to be more successful than those who will "learn on the job' because by the time they get acquainted fully with processes, the enterprise may have encountered considerable difficulties (Kinyanjui and Manguti, 1997).

Experience as a factor that determines entrepreneurial behaviour is pertinent in determining him direction the enterprise will take. Hands-on experience will facilitate processes like procurement of inputs, raw materials, market trends and customer relations (Maragia, 2003). Scolt (1986) attributes entrepreneur success to their astute use of experience and background.

2.5.10 Culture

The development of a culture is at individual, family, school, national and international levels. Culture is complex. It includes knowledge, customs, and habits acquired by man as a member of a society. Culture is the entire behaviour which members of a society acquire. It includes values, norms, and institutions and is passed over from one generation to another (McCormick, 2001).

Institutions have the role of shaping culture (Bwisa, 2000). A few studies conducted in Africa indicate that some cultures can create enabling environment for entrepreneurs. Casual research reveals that amongst Kenyan communities, some ethnic groups have more entrepreneurs who are concentrated all over the economy. McClelland suggests that language is a very crucial factor that influences an

---

39 McCormick. The Impact of Economic Reform on Entrepreneurial Activity: a theoretical Framework for Analyzing Small Enterprises.
40 Wickham. (1998). Strategic Entrepreneurship.

entrepreneur's direction. An example in this regard is of Kenyan Asian entrepreneurs who are in command of their business because of a strong culture and a strong language bond.

There is an assumption as societies grow and advance; they shift their patterns to adapt to new technologies that contribute to another stage of entrepreneurship. Cross-cultural studies have shown similarities among entrepreneurs. For example, in USA, the creation of patent rights is highly valued, hence the constitutional recognition of property rights. In Africa, scholars have found that entrepreneurial behavioural is affected by certain constraints, namely lack of experience in entrepreneurship, deficient ability to manage and strategize low levels of education, attention to changing trends of the society and economy which contribute to the drive to be successful.

2.5.11 Environment

Environment points at numerous kinds of external factors that affect a business operation but which are controllable –e.g. the ecological, geographical, political and economic contexts which impact on business operations. The environment thus refers to circumstances or conditions that surround somebody; the totality of circumstances, the combination of external physical conditions that affect the influence of growth, development and survival of organization, the complexity of social cultural conditions affecting the nature of an individual or a community (Richter, 1993).

Environment is used here to refer to the firm's local, national, international or global contexts. The entrepreneur's environment requires the availability of technology, combined with resources. Here technological environment refers to both hard ware and software, changing inputs into outputs. With a conducive environment, opportunities are provided for entrepreneurs to manipulate. Studies on Japan industry shows there are no large firms (webber, 1992).Rather; there is a combination of many small ones, which have specialized in different products. A study done in Kenya through the World Bank by Richter (1993) revealed that an entrepreneur needs a supportive and favourable business environment to facilitate progress. Sexton and smilor (1997) have expressed similar sentiments with regard to the entrepreneurial environment.

The context entrepreneurs face as they pursue their entrepreneurial dreams impact them both positively and negatively. The environmental condition alters activities of groaned in a particular country, posing new challenges and opportunities which are also seen as new drivers of an economy. The most critical of these environmental aspects are information revolution, technological advances and breakthroughs, globalization and demographics.

For example, acceleration information flow through Internet, radio, and mobile phones provides a practical solution to availing information at the touch of a button anywhere, anytime. An investor can log on to the Internet in Los Angeles at 2:00 am and the exchange rate for the yen, and correspond to a broker at the Nairobi Stock Exchange (NSE). A shopper can order goods without physically visiting the market place. The availability of information has radically altered the entrepreneurial behaviour response to the natural economy. This is described as the Information Age, where everything is linked to computers and telephone by means of modems.

Figure 7: New Venture creations

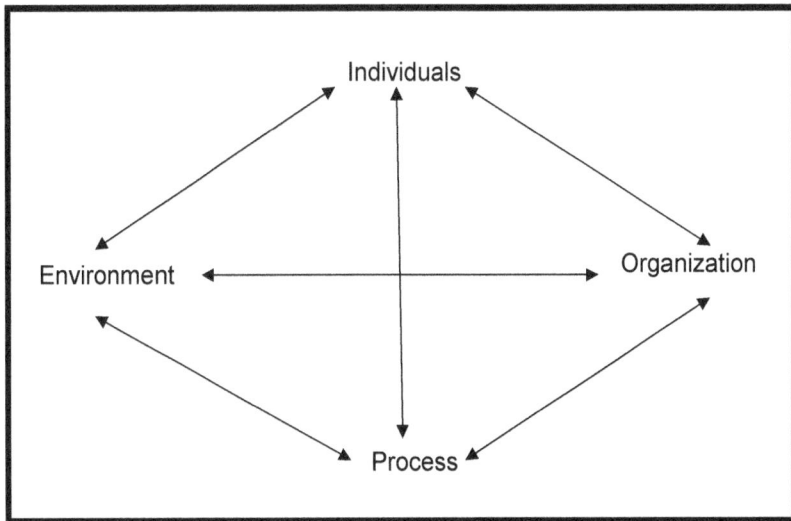

Source: *Gather W.B. (1985). "A Conceptual Framework for Describing the phenomenon of New Venture Creation," Academy of Management Review, Vol.10, No.4, p.68.*

According to Gartner (1985), a new venture has four dimensions:
1. Individuals(s) - the people involved in starting the venture.
2. Organization - the kind of firm that is started.
3. Environment - the situation surrounding and influencing the new organization.
4. The new venture process – the action s undertaken by the individual(s) to start the venture.

2.5.12 Gender

Gender is a domain of social practice. In business terms, it largely implies division of labour and determines activities within the household. It is one of the factors that impact negatively on the progress of entrepreneurs. A manifestation of who people are and what they do, gender can be linked to the awareness of women in development (scott,1986).In UK, statistics from the 1987 employment gazette show that females account for 45 percent of the employed population. Part-time female employment is 42 percent of all female employees, the service sector accounts for 65.7% of female employment (Scott).Discussions on gender often centre on equality of opportunity and elimination of all forms of discrimination for the girl child.

An unfortunate reality in Kenya is that women are an endangered group, going by the inequalities they face! Many Kenyan cultures exhibit imbalanced distribution of income to women, little or no access to productive inputs, lack of access to a competitive education and training and bias in labour market. All these combine to hinder the girl child from equal entrepreneurial opportunity. For example, in the baseline survey of (1999), 13.75% of women were found to have no formal education with the figure for men standing at just 6.8%. Consequently, more women are engaged in skilled activities, rendering them more susceptible to poverty. More obstacles come in the way of land ownership, which is still dominated by men because family land is registered in the name of the man of the house. Women have little claim to family property and control of productive resources (Sessional Paper No.3, 2004).

On the bright side, however, women's participation in MSE (ownership) has increased to 48% in recent years. A 1986 USA report on small business found that women-owned businesses were growing much faster than male owned business in the "traditional area of retail and service."

2.5.13 Infrastructure

Infrastructure is a primary driving force to the development of a country's competitive services. It includes sewage, telecommunication, roads, railways and electricity. Since independence in 1963, most Kenyan entrepreneurs reported 7% of problems related to transport. By 1995, this had gone up to 12%. It dropped to 7.2% by 1999 (baseline survey 1999).

A good infrastructure precipitates development and has a great effect in promoting competitive MSE sector growth by lowering the cost of conducting business. On the contrary, the public sector that is expected to provide momentum for growth is constrained by lack of efficiency, poor services and goods of unreliable quality.

Thus, there is an acute need to have efficient and adequate infrastructural facilities. These are essential for the growth of micro and small enterprises in Kenya (sessional paper No.2, 1992).According to sessional paper No.3 of 2004; the inadequacy of physical infrastructure affects the progress of MSEs greatly, thus constraining them from growth. For example, the state of many roads, railway network, and airports impacts negatively on the performance of MSEs.Needless to say that most MSEsdo not own land and their work sites are owned by influential individuals.

2.6 Conceptual Framework

The conceptual framework underpinning this work is small firm performance using the institutional economic framework (North, 1990). The theoretical framework linking entrepreneurship and economic growth is provided by the institutional theories of industrial evolution (North, 1990; jovahovic, 1982; Erickson &Pakes, 1995; Audretsch, 1995; Hopehayn, 1992; lambson, 1991 and Klepper, 1996).

The old traditional theories suggest that entrepreneurship will retard economic growth. The new theories give a completely opposite position that entrepreneurship will stimulate and generate growth. The discrepancies lie in the context of the theory where old traditional theory and new knowledge plays no role; static efficiency and ability to exhaust scale economies dictates growth.

In comparing and contrasting these positions, we note that the new theories are more dynamic in nature and emphasize the role that knowledge plays. Knowledge is known to be inherently uncertain, asymmetric and associated with high costs of transation, hence divergences that come in the expected values of new ideas. Economic agents are therefore forced to leave an incumbent firm in favour of starting a firm to tap incentives in an attempt to commercialize the perceived value of their knowledge (jovahovic, 1982).In entrepreneurship is found a vehicle where radical ideas are implemented. These evolutionary theories are focused i.e. on change as a central phenomenon. Innovative activities are some of the central manifestations of change. The industrial changes are linked to innovation and such dynamic performance in regions and even entire economies are all linked to the way innovation potentials are tapped (North, 1990).

North (1990) argues that institutions (macro economic/political) are analogous to the rules of the game in a competitive team sport. The purposes of the rules are to define the method and the way the game is played. The objective of the team (MSEs in this case) within the set goals is to win the game (how to do things, firm level institutions).

Figure 8: Baseline conceptual Model

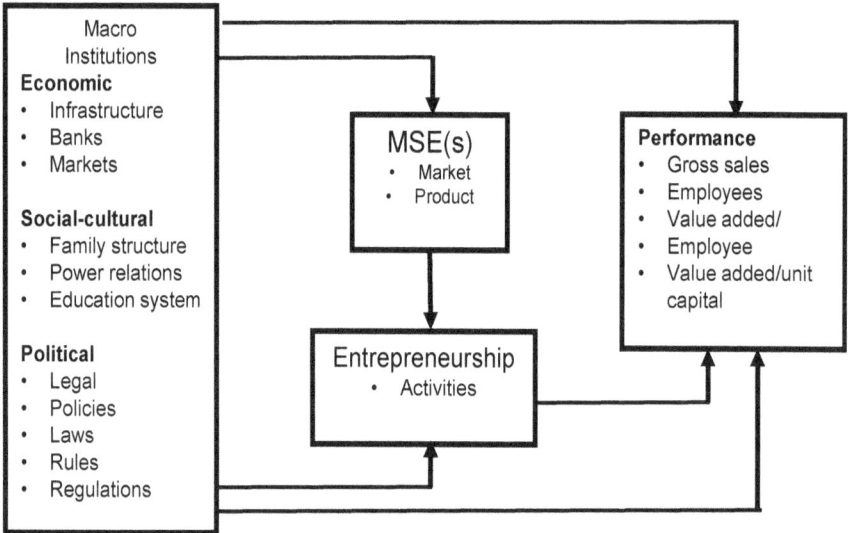

Source: *North Douglas. (1990). Institutions, Institutional Change and Economic Performance: Political Economy of Institutions and Decisions, Cambridge University Press*

According to Audretsch (1995), many firms are started to capitalize on the distinctive knowledge about innovation that originates from the sources outside of an industry's leaders. Jovahovic (1982) presents a model where new firm entrepreneurs face costs, which are random and also differ across the firms.

The central feature of the model is that the new firm does not know its cost function, that is, its relative efficiency. Thus, Jovahovic (1992) assumes that the entrepreneurs are unsure about the ability to manage a new firm, making them to doubt own success prospects. However,in pursuit of these activities (entrepreneurship) – which means among other things, understanding the products, market prices, machinery, handling employees appropriately – they enhance the image of the firm and create and sustain credibility amongst financial institutions. Hence, entrepreneurship is the commitment to evolve and grow an enterprise whereby things need not be created a new but where things are done innovatively and differently. At this juncture an entrepreneur discovers their true ability in managerial competence and viable ideas on the market when the business is established. Hence, the entrepreneur expands the scale of their business.

Thus, Jovanovich's model is a theory where efficient firms grow and survive and inefficient ones decline and fail. It emerges therefore that the role of micro small enterprises to the market is to set motion to new firms entering he industry and many firms exiting. Here, small firms begin a small scale of output which is started on the desire to appropriate the expected new economic knowledge. For example, the firm is likely to grow to survival based on the strategy of compensating factor, making it to discover the viability of its product.

By serving as an agent of change, entrepreneurship provides an essential source of new ideas and experimentation that otherwise would remain untapped in the economy. Its impact is manifested in growth levels of the firm in the region and nationally (Jovanovich, 1982).

2.7 Performance Measures

According too North (1990),performance is how a firm does when measurements are undertaken. Accordingly,it refers to how well the firm is doing in terms of measurable parameters like gross sales per employee, value added per employee, value added per unit of capital, etc.

- Gross sales per employee refer to the total sales divided by the number of employees in the firm.
- Value added per unit of capital will mean total sales less total costs divided by the estimated value of the machines being used.
- Value added per employee means or refers to total sales less total costs divided by the number of employees.

In economic performance that is linked to activity, the hypothesis has two challenges:

- Economic performance and how it is measured and made operational.
- Which units of analysis should a positive relationship between entrepreneurship and economic performance be manifested?

From the discussion above, the uses are not independent of each other and the units of analysis have influenced the first question:

- The performance criteria
- Measure-growth, income, wages, survival, innovation and productivity.

Other performance measures include:
- Profitability
- Satisfaction (owners and employees).

It is important to observe that the typical performance measure is on *earnings* or income generated from owned firms while such measures of growth at individual level makes little sense (Jovanovich, 1982). According to Jovanovich, enterprise and establishment levels are measured by way of growth, typical employment growth, survival, profitability, exports, foreign direct investment, and levels of employment, compensation, innovation, creativity and productivity.

However, other scholars contend that it is difficult to ascertain and research on profitability, since many organizational records cannot be accessed, resulting therefore in accounting difficulties.

Although many studies have focused on innovative activities as a performance criterion, ACS, Andretsch and Feldman (1994), Andretsch and Feldman (1996) and Almeida and Kogut (1997) using different performance measures in units of analysis, gave compelling links between entrepreneurship and performance which also points to the robust relationship between measures of entrepreneurship and economic performance. This relationship is found to affect a broad spectrum of performance measures like employment, growth, firm survival, innovation, creativity, technological change, productivity increase, and exports.

Entrepreneurial behaviour is responsible for playing a key role in the building of the economy, political and social welfare and an environment that stimulates entrepreneurial dynamism (see Figure 9).

Figure 9: Entrepreneurial Dynamism

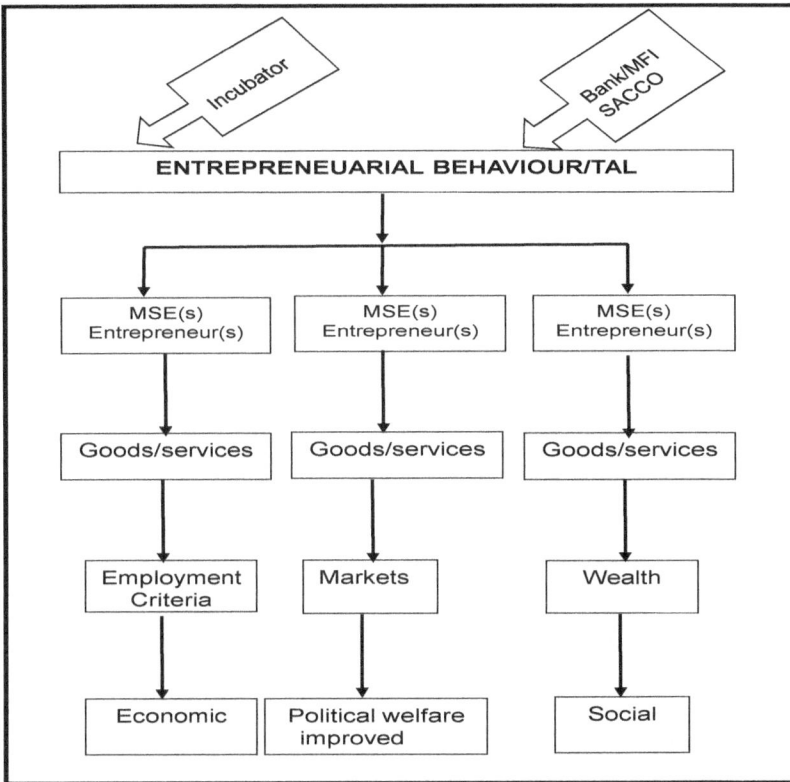

2.8 Institutions and Organizations

Institutions, according to North (1990), are responsible for providing structures to everyday life. They change the way societies evolve through time.

Institutions are understood in a broader sense so that it is adequately analyzed. The difference between an organization and an institution is in the fundamental influence in the evolution of such institution (North, 1990). According to McCormick, the New

Institutional Economics (NIE) is defined as a collection of perspectives. Different authors define institutions differently. Williamson (1975) and north (1990) focus on economics and political institutions while Grannovatter (1985, 1995) focuses on social and cultural institutions.

Pedersen and McCormick (1999) define institutions as a set of constraints that governs the behavioural relations amongst individuals and groups while North calls institutions rules of the game in a society. Such constraints are human-devised constraints that shape interaction amongst people.

According to Scott, the relationship between institutions and interest is explored to show that institutional features of organizational environments shape both goals and means of actors. In the work of Selznick, Institutionalisation is a process of instilling value, an adoptive vehicle shaped in reaction to the characteristics and commitments of participants and to influence constraint from the external environment (Scott, 1987).Scott further argues that institutions are technical instruments, designed as means to define goals that are subject to conscious design and intervention. The argument is based fundamentally on a share social reality i.e. a human construction for social interaction.

For Zucker (1993), emphasis is on institutionalisation as a process has continued to dominate the force of the mode is in the cognitive convictions they evoke, for example the "Black box" internalisation process of conformity. Empirically Zucker has demonstrated that behaviour is much more likely to be stable and conform to the requirements imposed by authoritative actors. Whereby authority is legitimated power or regulated power. Scott (1975, 56-63) in the work of March and Olsen (1984) pointed out that everything happening is not necessarily intended and the outcome may not be the result of a conscious decision process. This argument helps to account for some effects of institutional environment. Friendland and Alford (1987; 20) describe institutional as ends and shape the means by high interests are determined and pursued.[41]

It is argued that organizations do take a life of their own, irrespective of the desire of those presumably in control. And all institutions do so to some extent, presumably, but for some this fact is dominant. Basic to Selznick's view of organization is the distinction between the rational, means oriented, efficiency-guided of administration and the value laden adoptive, responsive process of institutionalization, taking on a distinctive character with natural growth. The administrative leader becomes a "statesman" using creativity to recognize and guide this process with a high sense of identity, purpose and commitment.

41   Friendland, Rodgers R.Alford. (1987),Bringing Society Back in Symbols,Structures and Institutional Contradiction, Centre for Advanced Studies in Behavioural Science, Stanford, Ca May 15-16.

Scott   W.Richard.(1982,1985,1987).Health   Care   organization   in 1980s,Conflict Levels of Rationality Regulators, Managers and professionals in the Medical Care Sector Organization: Rational, Natural and open System 2nd Ed.,Englewood Cliffs,NJ:Prentice – Hall.

Zucker Lynne G.(1977,1983, 1987). Institutional Theories of Organizations: The Role of Institutionalization in cultural persistence Americas. S. Review Organization as Institutions.

Williamson, Olivere. (1981, 1985).Economics of Organizations: The Transaction Cost Approach and Economics Institutions of Capitalism, American journal of Sociology, 87:548-577. New York: Free Press.

CHAPTER TWO

CASE STUDY OF KARIOBANGI LIGHT
INDUSTRIES

2.0 Introduction

The methodology used sought to put the research question into prospective and establish the connection between existence of entrepreneurial behaviour amongst micro and small enterprises in Kenya.

Both qualitative and quantitative techniques were used to collect and analyse the data. This is a departure from the conversational approaches that are either presented statistically (quantitative) or descriptive (qualitative).

The use of the two methods was a deliberate attempt to add value to the study of entrepreneurial behaviour while providing a creative and concrete contribution to body of knowledge in entrepreneurial behaviour amongst MSEs.

The research adopted a simple random sampling design. According to cooper Emory (1995),[1] 1 in random sampling each population element has an equal chance of being selected into the sample. It is also easy to implement with automatic dialling. However, one requires a list of population elements and it is likely to take more time to implement.

2.1 Brief Description of Research Site

The research site, Kariobangi South Light Industries (KSLI) is situated in the densely populated slum area east of Nairobi. It is in Kasarani Division of Nairobi province. The site was deliberately selected to study the entrepreneurial behaviour of the existing MSE entrepreneurs.

There is great diversity among Kenyans living in this area. Equally diverse are the industries they engage in. Many of those living here survive on less than a dollar a day and certainly enjoy low levels of financial services.

KSLI has a population of 350,625. It is 6662 feet above sea level and covers close to 5.5 km2 to the East of Nairobi. It is situated at 37° East and 1° north of Greenwich.

---

1   Cooper and Emory. (1995).Business Research Methods, IRWIN – Chicago: McGraw-Hill Co.

The area is served with electricity but has irregular supply of piped water. It is served by a main narrow and pot-holed tarmac road, Outer Ring road, which is the main bypass connecting Jomo Kenyatta International Airport to the busy Thika Road.

KSL borders a number of institutions. These include National Youth service Training college, the security printer De la Rue (currency printing), General Service Unit headquarters, East African Breweries and the middle class residential areas of Buru Buru and Komarock. It enjoys adequate transport means by Nissan *matatus*, mini buses, buses and a train service. The site therefore provides enormous opportunities to justify our choosing it as our study area.

Figure 10: Map of Nairobi (Source; Survey of Kenya)

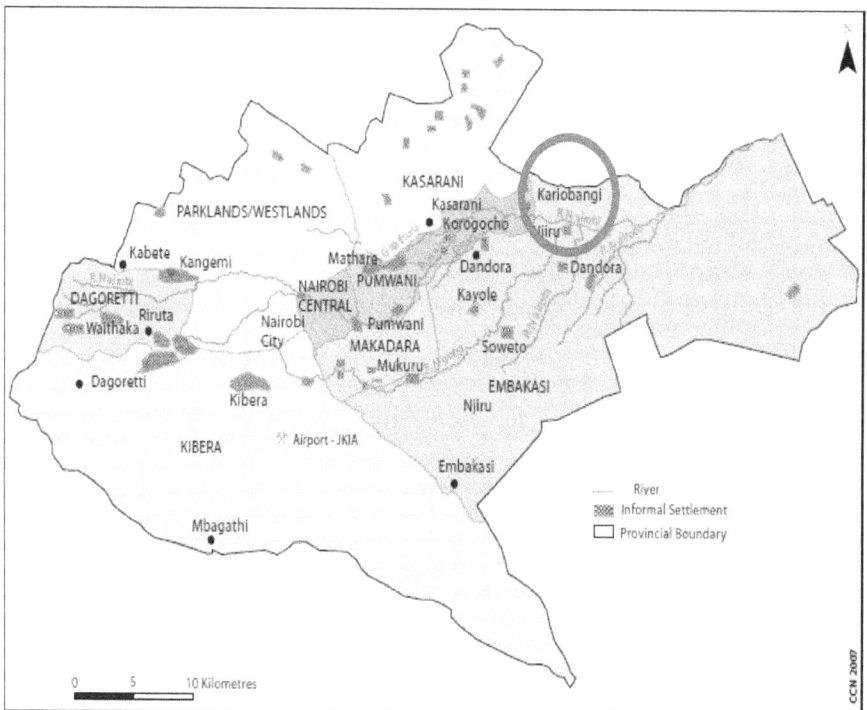

Figure 11: Map of Kenya (Source: Survey of Kenya)

2.2 Research Study Design

This study used a social survey method to collect data. This was considered necessary to utilize both quantitative and qualitative methods.

The qualitative approach was used particularly to supplement and strengthen the quantitative aspect and to provide an opportunity to the author to observe the entrepreneurial behaviour first-hand. Interview Schedules and Focus Group Discussions (FGD) were utilized.

There were a total of 170 respondents (MSE entrepreneurs) drawn from KSLI in East Nairobi – Kenya's second large slum area with a huge population of the unemployed. Those who are lucky to get employed earn less than one US dollar per day. Interviews were conducted using standard questionnaires aimed at probing into the phenomenon of entrepreneurial behaviour amongst MSEs in Kenya.

Data analysis was done using the statistical program for social sciences (SPSS).The author found it important to combine both quantitative and qualitative approaches to data collection and analysis. The benefit of this decision is that the qualitative aspect of data add value by enlightening quantitative data, making it more valuable (debus, 1996; Kinara, 2004).[2]

Pure statistically oriented (quantitative) approach to the study encompasses a two-way communication whereby dialogue is encouraged in data collection and analysis. During data collection, the researcher talked with the respondents making the whole exercise participative, thus creating curiosity in the respondents of how the discussion affects their day-to-day life. This interaction provided a perfect opportunity for the respondents to visualize the external environment with the researcher and with themselves.

It is assumed that conventional research approaches adopted methodologies which did not recognize the role of the respondents as answering questions from the researcher and taking keen interest to learn during the research session with a view of improving, reforming, and changing their business strategy.

According to cooper and Emory (1995), incorporating both qualitative and quantitative research aspects creates a shift in positions of both the researcher and researched, providing a mutual learning process in which both participants are enriched.

2.3 Sampling Frame

According to Levin (2001) and Rubin (2001, p.10), "A sample is a collection of some, but not all of the elements of the population" observed for the purposes of making inferences about the nature of the total population. It makes sampling cr6itical to the concept of social science research.

From the theory of sampling, relationships exist between the population and the samples drawn from it e.g. population mean or variance which is also known as population parameter. In sampling, a determination of observed differences between two samples is subjected to tests of significance and hypothesis (Cooper and Emory, 1995).

The respondents in this study were selected from entrepreneurs or respondent from light Industries in Kariobangi East of Nairobi and were designated for micro and small enterprises. The researchers went from door to door and requested the entrepreneurs to be interviewed, with the motive of achieving statistical inference. There were no lists of entrepreneurs or firms from which a sample was to be selected.

However, from the existing industries on the ground at the selected site a list of industries, establishments and jua kali hiring or employing

---

2   Kinara, E.O.(2004).PhD Thesis, "Mobilizing Savings of the Poor in addressing their Poverty of Financial Services: The Case for Kibera Slums Nairobi."

50 or less employees as contained in the policy guidelines of the Kenya Government,CBS and MSEs were useful for the purposes of this project.

The MSEs were categorized into four:
- Trade
- Manufacturing
- Construction
- Services

Thus, the entire population was about 445 plots employing between 5 and 50 employees in all the sub-sectors. A stratified sample of 170 entrepreneurs was selected.

According to the widely used rule of thumb, David and terell (1975) proposed a small sample size of 170. The number of respondents was distributed according to sub-sectors: Trade, manufacturing, construction and service.

2.4 Data Collection

In data collection, a structured questionnaire was used as an instrument to collect the data. Qualitative and quantitative data was collected through self-administered questionnaire by a questionnaire interview. This method was to facilitate increase in response rate and reduce or eliminate a language barrier that was expected of those respondents who do not know how to read and write. At times, the researcher enlisted an assistant to read the questions, simplify, and fill the blank spaces provided. The quantitative methods relied on the use of the questionnaire which was distributed to the respondents in their respective premises. The qualitative approach included focus group discussions (FGDs) and in-depth interviews (IDIs).

To obtain quantitative data for the purposes of the research, eight FGDs were conducted with entrepreneurs in Kariobangi South of Light industries. These were specifically organized for research purposes. Initially; they (respondents) were jittery since there is great suspicion among Kenyans regarding research, especially in an area like this, which has security problems. But we did explain our intention as being purely research. Those recruited to form discussion groups had experiences of harassment by various agencies, e.g. Local authorities, central government, and tax authorities.

The researcher sought consent from the respondents before interviewing them. They told the researcher that many people had disguised themselves as researchers only to use the information to penalize the respondents.

The FGDs were to improve responses, enhance consistency and obtain pertinent issues central to the study.

2.5 Data Analysis

The data is analysed and checked for competences. Indeed data is analysed through descriptive statistical by use of factor analysis models.

2.6 Data Analysis Techniques

The data analysis technique used was factor analysis as interdependent statistical techniques (Cooper and Emory, 1995). It was used to identify a set of dimensions observable in the variables by summarizing majority information in the original set of data into fewer factors.

Secondly, it was used to reduce large numbers of measures that were interrelated and caused multi-collinearity to a manageable number of factors which were not related and retained most of the information in the original data. According to cooper and Emory (1995), the predictor criterion relationship is found in the dependant situation replaced by a matrix of intercolleration among several variance, none of which is viewed as being dependent upon others.

Factors analysis has the advantage of being constructed as a new set of variables from the relationship in the correlation matrix. The most common approach is principal component analysis, realized by making new sets of composite variables or principal components which are not correlated with each other.

According to Cooper and Emory (1995) a numerical result from an example of a factor study is shown below.

Table 1

FACTOR MATRICES

Variable	Un-Rotated Factors			Rotated Factors	
	1	11	h²	1	11
A	.70	-40	65	.79	.15
B	.60	-50	61	.75	.03
C	80	-35	48	68	.10
D	50	-50	-50	06	.70
E	60	-50	61	13	.77
F	60	.60	72	07	.88
Eigen Value	2.18			1.39	
Percentage Variance	36.30			23.20	
Cumulative Percentage	36.30			59.50	

Factor analysis is best used for exploration, because new patterns can be detected in latent variables, discover new concepts and reduce data (Cooper and Emory). Factor analysis is good in taking hypothesis.

There were three steps followed:
- Calculation of correlation matrix between the factors for all pairs for which data exist.
- Factor analysis of the matrix by the principal components method.
- Selection of rotation procedure to clarify the factors and aid interpretation.

Interpretation: Varimax rotation appeared to clarify the relationship amongst variables, while the results are largely subjective (cooper and Emory 1995).

2.6.1 The Chi Square distribution

According to cooper and Emory (1995),[3] Chi Square is used to test whether the observation of sets of frequencies differs significantly from the expected frequencies. Some of the frequencies are treated as if they belong to a normal or continuous distribution when they actually belong to the binomial or discrete distribution.

In chi square tests, the results obtained do not always agree exactly with theoretical results expected and according to the rules of probability. Hence, why we need to know whether the observed frequencies differ significantly from expected frequencies. Such measures of discrepancy between observed and expected frequencies is supplied by x^2 statistics given by:

$$X^2 = \sum_{I=1}^{N} \frac{(O1-E1)^2}{Ei}$$

Example

Original definition of $X^2 = \frac{\sum (x-)^2}{2}$ is replaced by (1)

Where if the total of the frequency is N Then $\sum Oi = \sum Ei = N$

The equivalent expression to 1 is observed and the theoretical frequencies agree exactly.

3   8. Morgan (1998:12)

Uli (2002:46)

The Chi square test, also known as goodness of fit, is used to determine how well theoretical distribution is. For example, binomial, passion and normal fit the empirical distribution, e.g. those obtained from the sample data.

2.6.2 Significance Tests

The distributions are computed on the basis of a Hypothesis HO (NULL).The level OF 0.99 (X^2 0.95 OR X^2 0.99) which are the critical value that can be obtained from the table given the degrees of freedom at the 0.05 and 0.01 significance levels. HO is reflected or accepted. This procedure is called chi square test of hypothesis or significance.

2.6.3 Confidence Intervals for X^2

The definition of confidence intervals 95%, 99% are confidence limits and intervals for x^2 which is similar to normal distribution.

2.6.4 Analysis of Variance (ANOVA)

This is a test used to test for significance of the differences between more than two sample means. This analysis is useful in making inference about whether our samples are drawn from a population having the same mean (cooper and Emory, 1985). ANOVA is useful in a situation of comparison, for example in four different samples of company products where satisfaction is achieved; the means of more than two samples would be compared.

The concept of ANOVA is that the samples are drawn from a normal population and each has the same variance. Analysis of variance is based on a population. The steps of ANOVA are:
- Determine one estimate of the population variance from the variance from among the sample means.
- Compare the two estimates. If they are approximately equal in value, accept the null hypothesis.
- Determine a second estimate of population variance from the variance within the samples.

In ANOVA two estimates of the population variance are compared by computing the ratio called F, which is:
- First estimate of the population variance based on the variance among the sample means.
- Second estimate of the population variance within the samples.
- F. distribution has a pair of degrees of freedom, nominator and denominator.

2.7 Entrepreneur Attributes

2.7.1 Risk Taking

The literature reviewed for this study shows the risk taking variable as having three attributes i.e. selling at loss, credit sales and overstocking - for example an entrepreneur keeping huge stocks which are to end up as dead stock is a great risk in itself. It is that willingness on the part of the entrepreneur to give out goods to others on credit which can become a bad debt if the other party lacks the capacity to settle. Unstable price fluctuations sometimes make the entrepreneur to sell at a loss.

2.7.2 Innovativeness

When an entrepreneur starts something new, it is considered to have happened through innovativeness. It can be a new product or service. According to Drucker (1985), McDonald packaged the hamburger in a new style through innovation. Innovation implies an original idea, modification or improvement or both.

2.7.3 Knowledge of Results

The measuring of knowledge of results expected in an enterprise or venture by the entrepreneur is necessary, for example keeping financial records, stocks and statutory requirements (like taxes, books of accounts). For the entrepreneur to be able to plan the business to a satisfactory level, he should be result oriented.

2.7.4 Individual Responsibility

This calls for accountability to the businesses. The entrepreneur must be able to delegate some authority through prudent and sound management, for example floor management selling goods on credit to the regular and committed customer. Indeed, keeping of records and other documents is an important component in an undertaking.

2.7.5 Formal Education

Formal education in Kenya today is form four (4) as a high level of education in the formal education system.

2.7.6 Formal Training

Entrepreneurs with formal training have higher expectations of success. Training is a vital tool in their hands to knock down obstacles on their way to successful business enterprises.

2.7.7 Experience

Entrepreneurs who are aged 30 years and above are more settled to start and manage a business. Studies indicate a positive relationship between age and experience (Drucker, 1985).such settled entrepreneurs are likely to have many years of social experience, economic and political encounters. Moreover, they have managed family commitments and obligations and can thus concentrate and accord more time to a successful business venture. In addition, such an entrepreneur will likely possess rich experience from his profession.

2.7.8 Access to Resources and Credit

Many MSEs have a problem finding qualified staff. More often than not there is a very high incidence of staff turnover.

To get access to credit requires collateral, which many entrepreneurs lack. This makes it impossible to procure any loan from the bank. Many banks are reluctant to embrace MSEs in their lending policy because such institutions are not supported by government legal and regulatory frameworks.

2.7.9 Motivation

Many entrepreneurs are motivated to enter business because of the desire to be independent from formal employment. Other could have come out of formal and regular employment to make profits and earn more income.

2.8 Behavioural Characteristics

These include risk taking, innovativeness, knowledge of results and individual responsibility.

2.9 Determining Factors

These were found to be motivation, access to resources, experience, training, formal education, formal training and experience.

2.10 Hypothesis Tested

1. Entrepreneurs with high levels of formal education (having completed form 4 schooling) will show great interest and commitment towards entrepreneurial behaviour as compared with those with low levels of education.

Hypotheses:

   i. Entrepreneurs with high levels of formal education will show greater inclination towards risk taking as compared to those with low levels of formal education.

ii. Entrepreneurs with high levels of formal education will show greater inclination towards innovativeness as compared to those with low levels of formal education.

iii. Entrepreneurs with high levels of formal education will show greater interests and concern for knowledge of results as compared to the ones with low levels of formal education.

iv. Entrepreneurs with high levels of formal education will show a greater sense of individual responsibility as compared to the ones with low levels of formal education.

2.

i. Entrepreneurs who have prior training relevant to the running of the present business will show a greater need for knowledge as compared to the ones with no training or with training in a field not relevant to the present business.

ii. Entrepreneurs who have prior training relevant to the running of the present business will show greater interest towards innovativeness as compared to the one with no training or with training in another field not relevant to the present business.

iii. Entrepreneurs who have prior training relevant to the running of the present business will show greater tendency towards risk taking as compared to the one with no or other training in another field not relevant to the present business.

iv. Entrepreneurs who have prior training relevant to the running of the present business will show greater entrepreneurial behaviour as compared to those with little or no training.

v. Entrepreneurs who have prior training relevant to the running of the present business will show a greater degree of responsibility than those with no training or with other training in another field not relevant to the present business.

3. Entrepreneurs with experience will show more entrepreneurial behaviour as compared to those with little or no experience at all. The following were used to test the derived hypothesis:

i. Entrepreneurs with experience will show greater tendency towards risk taking as compared to those with little or no experience.

ii. Entrepreneurs with experience will show a greater inclination towards innovativeness as compared to those with little or no experience.

iii. Entrepreneurs with relevant business experience will show a greater desire for knowledge of result as compared to those with little or no experience.

iv.   Entrepreneurs with relevant business experience will show a greater degree of individual responsibility as compared to those with little or no experience.

4. Entrepreneurs with greater access to credit will show greater entrepreneurial behaviour as compared to those with little or no access to resources. Hypothesis tested were:

   i.   Entrepreneurs who have access to credit will show greater tendency towards risk taking than those with no access to the credit.

   ii.   Entrepreneurs who have access to credit will show greater tendency towards innovativeness than those with no such facilities.

5. Entrepreneurs with great achievement motives will show greater entrepreneurial behaviour than those with low levels of achievement motive. Hypothesis testing encompassed the following:

   i.   Entrepreneurs who have stronger achievement motives will show greater risk taking ability than those with low levels of achievement motives.

   ii.   Entrepreneurs who have stronger achievement motives will show greater innovativeness than those with low levels of achievement motives.

   iii.   Entrepreneurs who have stronger achievement motives will show a strong desire for knowledge of result than those with low levels of achievement motives.

   iv.   Entrepreneurs who have stronger achievement motives will show greater responsibility than those with low levels of achievement motives.

2.11 Dependent Variables

These were identified as risk taking, innovativeness, individual responsibilities; individual responsibility and knowledge of results. The influencing factors are independent of each other and hence affect the dependent variables above.

CHAPTER THREE

DATA ANALYSIS AND FINDINGS

3.0 Introduction

This chapter presents analysis of the findings of the study as well as interpretation of the results. The study has utilized both quantitative and qualitative analysis to get an in-depth understanding of the findings of the study. The results of both structured and unstructured questionnaires have been integrated with findings of interviews and observations that were used as supplements to gain a deeper understanding of the variables examined.

3.1 Response Rate

Out of 170 questionnaires distributed to respondents, 133 were filled appropriately and returned, a constituting 78% return rate.22% of the respondents were reluctant to participate in the survey citing confidentiality in spite of efforts made to explain the purpose. Although the initial sample size was 450, equivalent to the number of plots in KSLI, the field survey discovered that no businesses were conducted in some premises.

Figure 12: Response Rate

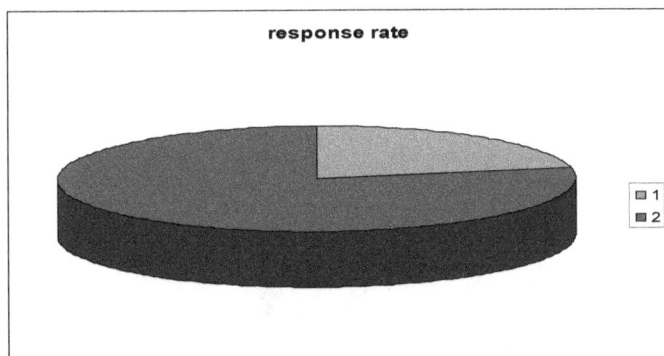

3.2 Data Analysis

The data collected was analysed using descriptive statistics as well as factor analysis. Descriptive statistics entailed frequency distribution and percentages. Factor analysis entailed measures of association and strength of those factors that affect entrepreneurship. The result of this study is presented in two parts. The first presents the findings on the profile of MSEs studied in KSLI. The second part addresses the findings on the objectives of the study.

3.3 Overview of the Profiles of MSE(s) and Respondents

(a) Respondent details

The respondents comprised of business proprietors (68.9%) or other staff (31.1%). The other staff demonstrated a capacity to answer all questions posed. Of those who responded, 72.1% were male and 27.9 female.

Table 2: Positions that Respondents hold in the business

	Frequency	Percent	Valid percent	Cumulative percent
Valid	91	68.4	68.9	68.9
Proprietor	41	30.8	31.1	100
Others	132	99.2	100.0	
Total	1	.8		
Missing system	100.0	100.0		
Total				

Source: *Field Survey 2005*

Figure 13: Respondents

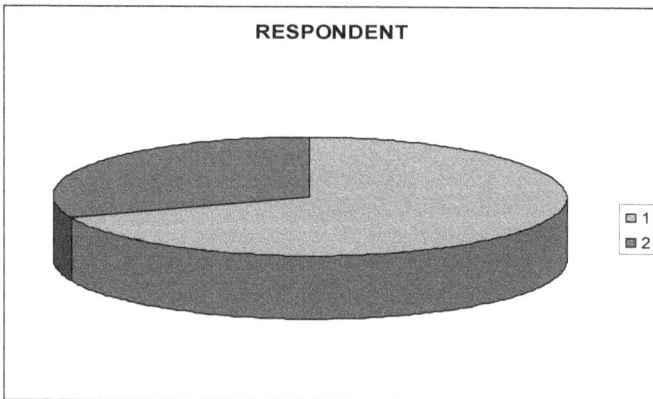

Table 3: Gender of the Respondents

		Frequency	Percent	Valid percent	Cumulative percent
Valid	Male	93	69.9	72.1	72.1
	Female	36	27.1	27.9	100
	Total	129	97.0	100	
Missing system		4	3.0		
Total		133	100		

Source: *Field Survey 2005*

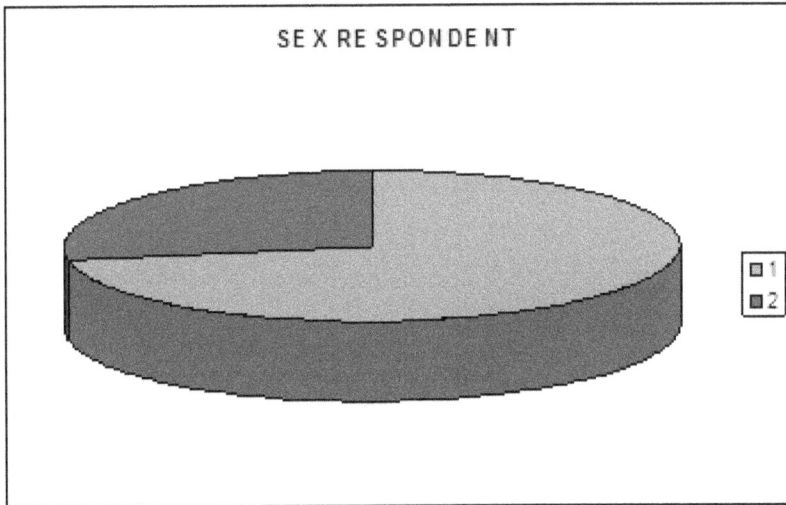

Figure 14: Gender of Respondents

Table 4: Age of the Respondents

	Frequency	Percent	Valid Percent
Valid Below 25			
26-35	9	6.8	6.9
36-45	41	30.8	31.3
46-55	41	30.8	31.3
Over 56	32	24.1	24.4
Total	8	6.0	6.1
Missing system	131	98.5	100.0
Total	2	1.5	
	133	100.0	

Source: *Field Survey 2005*

The age of the respondents ranged from below 25 years to over 56 years. 69.5% were aged below 46 years of age as depicted in Table 3

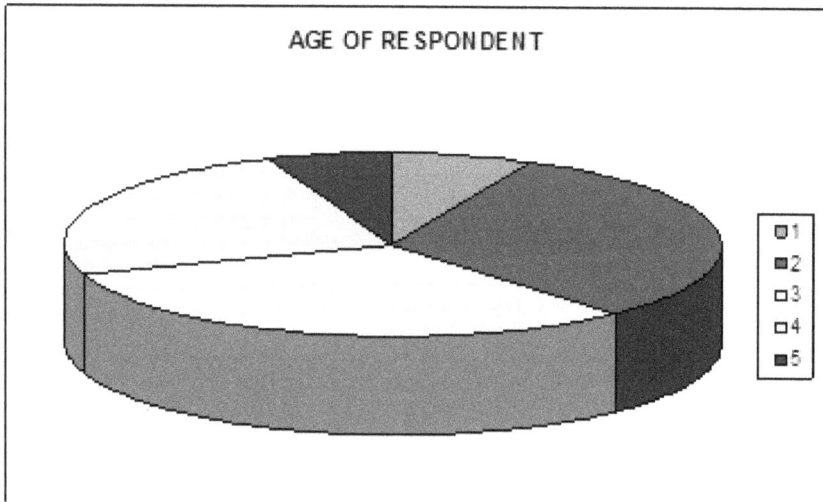

Figure 15: Age of Respondents

Table 5: Education level of Respondents

	Frequency	Percent	Valid Percent	Cumulative Percent
Valid				
Primary	3	2.3	2.3	2.3
Secondary	49	36.8	37.1	39.4
Tertiary	38	28.6	28.8	68.2
University	42	31.6	31.8	100.0
Total	132	99.2	100	
Missing system	1	.8		
Total	133	100.00		

Source: *Field Survey 2005*

The level of education among the respondents was quite good. Only 2.3 % had primary school education while the rest had secondary education and above. Those with university level of education comprised 31.8% of the sample while secondary education holders were a slight majority at 37.1%. These results indicate that a vast majority of the respondents are well educated.

Figure 16: Education Level Of Respondents

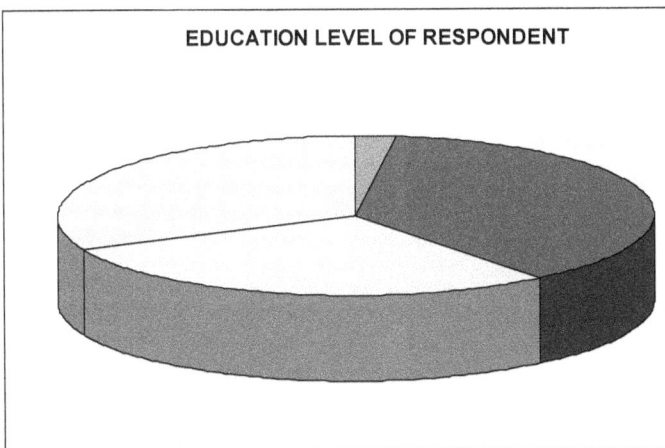

EDUCATION LEVEL OF RESPONDENT

(b) Type of Businesses

Table 6: Type Of Business

		Fre-quency	Percent	Valid Per-cent	Cumulative Per-cent
Valid	Trade	51	38.3	38.3	38.3
	Manufactur-ing	57	42.9	42.9	81.2
	Construc-tion	7	5.3	5.3	86.5
		9	6.8	6.8	93.2
		9	6.8	6.8	
	Bar/Hotel/Restaurant	133	100.0	100.0	100.0
	Services				
	Total				

Source: *Field Survey 2005*

The businesses were distributed among trade, manufacturing, construction, bar/hotel/restaurant and services. The majority however engage in some form of manufacturing which accounted for 42.9%,followed by trade that comprised 38.3%.

Figure 17 Type of Business

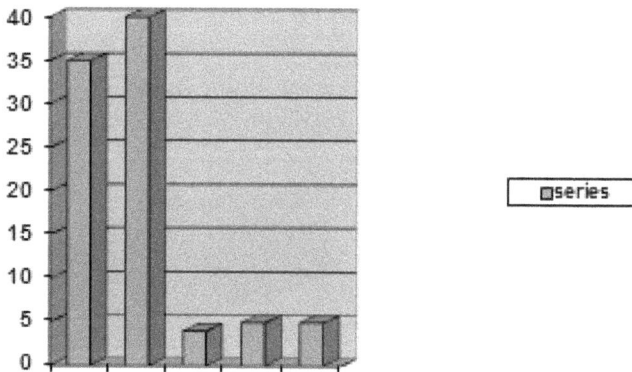

Table 7: Number of Employees per MSE

	Frequency	Percent	Valid Per-cent	Cumulative Per-cent
Valid Trade	51	38.3	38.3	38.3
Manufacturing	57	42.9	42.9	81.2
Construction	7	5.3	5.3	86.5
Bar/hotel/restaurant	9	6.8	6.8	93.2
Services	9	6.8	6.8	
Total	133	100.0	100.0	100.0

Source: *Field Survey 2005*

The majority of the enterprises had more than ten employees (36.6%). A good number (35.1%) had between 3 and 5 employees as indicated above.

Figure 18: Number of Employees per MSE

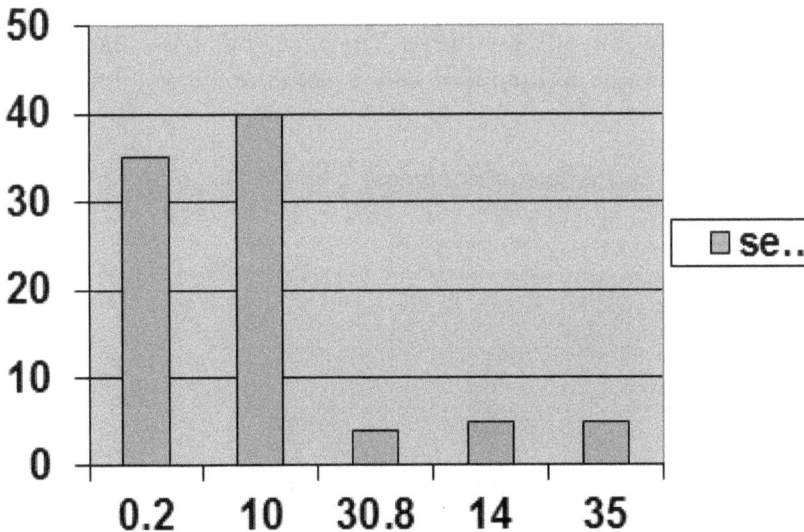

Table 8: Period in this Type of Business

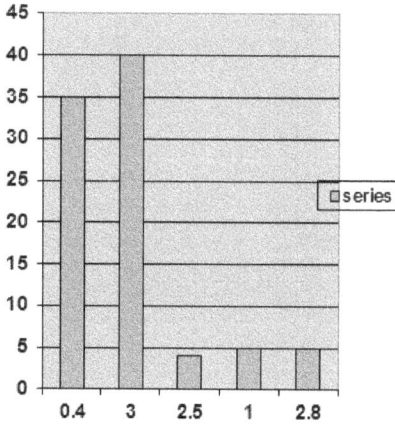

Source: *Field Survey 2005*

The length of experience of the respondents in their current type of businesses ranged from two to over ten years.36.4% had 2-5 years experience in the current business. The fact that 25% had over 10 years in the same line of business shows some resilience among these entrepreneurs.

Figure 19: Period in this line of Business

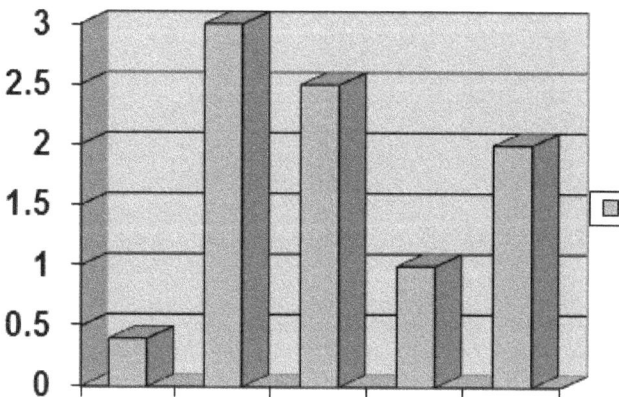

(c) Data Presentation

The most significant results are that only four factors determine entrepreneurial behaviour among MSEs in Kenya. These are the need to supplement income; availability of credit; desire to generate wealth and retrenchment of employees both in the public and private sectors. The three dominant constraints of entrepreneurs are access to credit; selling of products and poor communication.

To overcome these constraints, entrepreneurs have employed the following dominant strategies: selling on credit and products/services branding. As expected the drivers, dominant factors and strategies employed by entrepreneurs reflect the economic, social and political environment prevailing in Kenya.

A large proportion of the population in Kenya lives below the poverty line. Indeed political figures indicate that 56 percent live in poverty. The situation on the ground could be worse. In addition to poverty, this has been mounting pressure on the government to downsize and right size the civil service. Ordinarily this means sacking or compulsorily retiring civil servants so that the pressure on the exchequer is reduced. The main proponents of such radical policies are the World Bank and IMF. The motivation is to achieve economic stability and growth by placing a lid on public debt and deficits, interest rates, inflation and hence avoiding economic recession.

When viewed against the above background, the results of this study are not very surprising indeed; they corroborate the findings of similar studies elsewhere. Our major contribution therefore lies in further confirming the already known unique characteristic of entrepreneurs-innovation against an environment characterized by uncertainty, hardship and agony, and its absence among MSEs in Kenya.

3.4 Findings on the Objectives of the Study

(a) Factors that determine Entrepreneurial Behaviour amongst MSEs in Kenya.

The results of this study showed that from a list of ten factors believed to influence entrepreneurial behaviour only four are important in the MSEs sampled. These are the need to supplement income; availability of credit; the desire to generate wealth and retrenchment. Table 4.8 below provides a summary of the factor analysis results using principal components.

Table 9 Component Transformations matrix

Component	1	2	3	4
1.Supplementary Income	0.869	0.384	0.238	0.203
2. Credit availability	0.110	0.752	0.603	0.244
3.Generation of wealth	0.027	0.104	0.477	0.872
4.Retrenchment	0.182	0.526	0.594	0.372

Rotation Method: Varimax with Kaiser – Normalization

Using the component matrix, we identified the first component as the need to supplement income. This factor is positively correlated to components 2, 3 and 4, which are availability of credit; desire to generate wealth and retrenchment, respectively. The second component was highly loaded on the desire to be one's own boss and the availability of credit. Due to a higher loading on the latter in the rotated matrix compared to the former, we interpreted it as availability of credit. Moreover this component is highly correlated with failure to secure a job than the attraction to higher income or profit. The third component had a high load on the desire to generate wealth factor compared to the attraction to a higher income or profit. The third component had a high load on the desire to generate wealth factor compared to the attraction to a higher income or profit and failure to secure a job. We therefore interpreted it to be the desire to generate wealth. The fourth component was easy to interpret. It had the highest and conspicuous loading of 0.917 on retrenchment. The next positively correlated factor was only 0.404 on the failure to secure a job factor. We therefore identified it as retrenchment.

Thus, the results of this study indicate that the harsh economic environment and the liberalization of the Kenyan economy have driven entrepreneurial behaviour among MSEs in Kenya. The need to make ends meet is very strong among Kenyans in general. This emboldens them to face the harsh economic environment with determination, desperation and the strong will to generate income. Since there are a few jobs available, many qualified Kenyans are unemployed. This makes self-employment or entrepreneurship the alternative opportunity.

In order to undertake any business venture, finance is an important factor and also a major constraint to entrepreneurs. This study found that availability of credit is the second most important factor determining entrepreneurial behaviour among MSEs in Kenya. This means that if financial constraints can be eliminated, then more business ventures can be established, investments increased and the economy grow. The finance growth nexus is an old theme in development economics. Access to credit by MSE is known to be especially difficult in Kenya. Commercial banks favour large and well-established firms. Thus, MSEs face a big constraint in establishing and expanding their business. Alternative forms of finance are important though the amount of credit obtained from such sources is comparatively small.

The impact of retrenchment on the income of individuals and families in Kenya has been significant. Many individuals lost their jobs without any alternative source of income. Many of those affected by retrenchment had families and other dependants. Others had acquired loans secured by their pay slips. The harsh reality of losing a stable source of income with no possibility of landing another drove even the faint-hearted into entrepreneurship. Many of the newly created MSEs are a reaction to losing or the possibility of losing a job through retrenchment or otherwise.

In summary, while the factors that drive entrepreneurs are universal, the specific milieu within which entrepreneurs emerge and drive differ across place, space and time. In this study, we examined the dominant factors driving entrepreneurial behaviour among MSEs in Kenya. The evidence from this study indicates that the harsh economic environment in Kenya has been solely responsible for the observed entrepreneurial behaviour. The results suggest that if the majority of the entrepreneurial behaviour. The results suggest that if the majority of the entrepreneurs were offered a good job (i.e. a job with a good income) they could easily abandon their ventures. This leaves one to wonder whether there is an entrepreneurial culture in Kenya. Moreover, is the failure of MSEs to access credit further manifestation of this problem of lack of a culture of entrepreneurship? Ordinarily, one would expect that if indeed one is an entrepreneur, then the power and charm of the particular innovation to be undertaken could easily convince lenders to loosen purse strings. That this is indeed not the case seems to confirm our fears. Also, historical evidence from the corporate sector gives stronger evidence that in Kenya finance or credit is not a constraint. Evidence of share over-subscriptions on the Nairobi Stock Exchange confirms.

(b) *Constraints on Entrepreneurial Behaviour amongst MSEs*

There are three major constraints on entrepreneurs in Kenya. The first is access to credit. Since the problem of access to credit has already been discussed in (a) above, we shall discuss the other factors – selling of products (demand) and poor infrastructure.

The problem of selling of products or demand is a symptom of the underlying poverty among large segments of the Kenyan population and a lack of entrepreneurship culture. On one hand, poverty robs individuals of purchasing power. People cannot demand the products and services offered by entrepreneurs. On the other hand, inability to sell one's product is a sign of an inherent lack of innovativeness among MSEs. The market for their products has been essentially local. One is thus left sceptical of the idea that such products cannot find a market outside Kenya or in other strategic regions within the country.

The third major constraint on entrepreneurship was identified as poor infrastructure (road and telephone).Considering current developments in the mobile telephone sub-sector; this is no longer a serious problem, at least in Kenya. The road network in the country is generally poor.

However, it does not constraint innovative MSEs that can and have turned it into an opportunity. Since most of the MSEs sampled ranked poor infrastructure as one of the major constraints to entrepreneurship, it only goes to confirm our fears – the absence of an entrepreneurial culture in Kenya.

In summary, the three, main constraints to entrepreneurship among the MSEs in Kenya appear to be access to credit, selling of products/ services and poor infrastructure. However, a deeper analysis of these factors reveals that they are only symptoms of a more fundamental constraint – lack of entrepreneurial culture among MSEs.

(c) *Marketing Strategies of MSEs*

MSEs in Kenya predominantly use two marketing strategies namely credit selling and product branding. As a strategy for selling products, credit sales are commonly used when there are so many competitors compared to customers in a given market or niche. The motivation is to push products onto customers with the aim of increasing sales volumes. The strategy is used when there is low or deficient demand.

The principal causes of deficient or low demand in Kenya are poverty, unemployment and underemployment and poor remuneration. The net result is the low purchasing power of a significant cross section of the population. Therefore; the fact that MSEs in Kenya use credit sales simply confirms the low purchasing power among Kenyans and the thin market for their products. This is a situation where everyone is desperately trying to sell something to someone else who is unwilling to buy, for reasons that are not difficult to guess.

Under a competitive business environment backed by effective demand, branding could have been the predominant strategy employed by MSEs to market their products. In the light of the foregoing discussion, it is not surprising that credit selling foreshadows branding as a marketing strategy. Our result suggested that branding might not be a dominant strategy as such among MSEs.

In summary, we find that credit selling is the strategy used to market the products of MSEs in Kenya. Such a strategy reflects the harsh economic environment within which MSEs have mushroomed. It also reinforces our argument that many MSEs were set up as a reaction to retrenchment or a possibility of the same or other potential threats to one's income but not as a manifestation of the existence of an entrepreneurial culture in Kenya.

(d) Educational and Entrepreneurial Behaviour

To examine the relationship between education and entrepreneurial behaviour we formulated and tested the following hypotheses. We used the X^2 test in each case, and we rejected all the null hypotheses of independence.

(a) Ho: There is no difference between the level of risk-taking and the level of education of the entrepreneurs.

The computed X^2-statistical was 31.01. When we compared the computed value to the critical value $(X^2 = 7.814)$ (3df) at 95% confidence interval, we rejected the null hypothesis. Therefore, the level of education of an entrepreneur influences the amount and type of risk undertaken.

The results indicate that the 40 percent (53) of the entrepreneurs with high level education (secondary education and above) are high-risk takers while the majority (60 percent) are low risk takers. Among those with primary level education, half of them are high-risk takers and the other half are low takers. Thus, education improves an entrepreneur's sensitivity to and choice of risks. Educated entrepreneurs are risk averse.

(b) Ho: There is no difference between the levels of innovativeness and the level of education of the entrepreneurs

The computed X2 statistic was 28.34. When we compared this to the critical value (of 7.814) (3df), we rejected the null hypothesis. The level of education is a determinant of the innovativeness of the entrepreneur.

In particular, only 32 percent of the entrepreneurs with high level of education have a high inclination towards innovation. However, 68 percent of the entrepreneurs with a high level of education have a low inclination toward innovation. The entrepreneurs with a low level of education were evenly distributed between low and high inclination toward innovation. A possible explanation for these results is that innovation is expensive. Since many MSEs do not have access to credit, their aspirations to innovate are dampened.

(c) Ho: There is no Difference between the level of education and concern for knowledge of results by the entrepreneurs

This hypothesis was not supported by data. We found the computed X^2statistic (32.81) to be greater than the critical value (7.814).The results demonstrate that entrepreneurs with a high level of education tend to be more concerned about the results of their ventures than those with low or no education. Over 45 percent (69%) of entrepreneurs with high level of education showed high concern for knowledge of results. There is no difference among entrepreneurs with low or no formal education concerning the results of their business activities.

(d) Ho: There is no difference between the level of education and the sense of responsibility of the entrepreneurs.

The computed X^2 statistical was 32.43. When compared to the critical value of 7.814 we rejected the null hypothesis. The results indicated that entrepreneurs with a high level of education showed a high sense of responsibility compared to those with a low level of education. On the whole, 68 percent of the entrepreneurs with a high level of education demonstrated a high sense of responsibility.

For entrepreneurs with a low level of education, 50 percent had a high sense of responsibility and the rest a low sense of responsibility.

The level of education influences significantly the behaviour of an entrepreneur. Evidence suggests that the level of innovation, concern about knowledge of results and the sense of responsibility. In particular, there is a strong relationship between an entrepreneur's level of education and matters like selling strategy, formation of new ventures, keeping financial records, accountability, and delegation. Entrepreneurs with high levels of education will show a greater tendency toward record keeping, delegation of duty and an appropriate selling strategy.

(e) Training and Entrepreneurial Behaviour

We formulated and tested the following five hypotheses to study the impact of training on the behaviour of the entrepreneur. We applied a chi-square test at 95% confidence interval on all hypotheses. The results are presented below.

(a) Ho: There is no difference between the level of training and the entrepreneurs concern for knowledge of results.

The computed X^2 statistic was 21.19 against the critical value of 3.841 (1df).Therefore, we rejected the null hypothesis. The results further showed that 69 percent of trained entrepreneurs had a high concern for knowledge of results and only 31 percent had a low concern for results. Among entrepreneurs with no training (39 percent of the respondents), 27% had a high concern for knowledge of results; the remaining 12% did not.

(b) Ho: There is no difference between the level of training and the level of innovativeness of the entrepreneurs.

We tested hypothesis with a computed X^2 static of 20.96 against the critical value of 3.841.Therefore, we rejected the null hypothesis. While the percentage of entrepreneurs with training who showed greater interest in innovation (20%) was higher than those entrepreneurs without training (13%), the proportion of those who had low interest in innovation was higher (42%) for trained and non-trained (27%) entrepreneurs. Thus; training seems to have little impact of innovation or the tendency to innovate. A possible reason could be lack of capital as a consequence of inaccessible credit.

(c) Ho: There is no difference between the level of training and the tendency toward risk-taking behaviour of entrepreneurs.

The computed X^2 statistic was 23.17.This exceeds the critical value of 3.841.Therefore, we rejected the null hypothesis. Further analysis of the results indicated that 37 percent of entrepreneurs (those with training) showed a low tendency towards risk-taking compared to 23 percent of the entrepreneurs without training and who showed a low tendency towards risk-taking. Taken together these results support the assertion that entrepreneurs are risk averse, contrary to popular notion that they are risk-seekers.

(d) Ho: There is no difference between the level of training and the level of concern with knowledge of results of the entrepreneurs.

Using the X^2test we obtained a computed statistic of 24.63 against the critical value of 3.841. The null hypothesis was rejected. The results indicate that 54 percent of entrepreneurs, trained and not trained respectively showed a high concern for knowledge of results. While 7 percent and 4 percent of entrepreneurs, trained and not trained, respectively showed low concern for knowledge of results. This means that training increases the entrepreneurs concern for results from the business.

(e) Ho: There is no difference between level of training and the tendency toward greater responsibility of the entrepreneurs

The computed X^2 statistic is 23.36. This exceeds the critical value of 3.841 (1df).Therefore we rejected the null hypothesis. The results suggest that training improves the entrepreneur's tendency toward greater responsibility. Indeed,42 percent and 27 percent of entrepreneurs, trained and untrained respectively, showed a high degree of responsibility. However, 20 percent and 13 percent of entrepreneurs, trained and untrained, respectively demonstrated a low degree of reasonability.

(f) Experiences and Entrepreneurial Behaviour

This section examines the impact of an entrepreneur's experience on risk-taking, innovativeness, knowledge of results, and the level of responsibility of the entrepreneur. We formulated and tested the hypotheses below using the chi-square test at 95 percent confidence interval. We rejected all the null hypotheses.

(a) Ho: There is no difference between the level of experience and the level of risk-taking of the entrepreneurs

The computed X^2 static is 12.615. This exceeds the critical value of 7.814(3 df). Therefore, we rejected the null hypothesis. The results indicate that more experienced entrepreneurs (with 8 years and above) and newly created ventures (<2 years) have a low tendency toward high risk-taking behaviour. Only 24 percent of all entrepreneurs fell in the above category; whereas entrepreneurs between 2-7 years of experience constituted 36 percent of all respondents. On the other hand, only 16 percent of entrepreneurs with 8 and above years of experience or less than 2 years of experience had a low tendency toward risk-taking; whereas 24 percent consisted of entrepreneurs with 2-7 years of experience who have a high tendency toward risk-taking. Overall, these results seem to suggest that entrepreneurs are risk seekers. All entrepreneurs, irrespective of years of experience, tend towards high risk than low risk ventures.

(b) Ho: There is no difference between the level of experience and the tendency toward innovative of the entrepreneurs.

The results of the chi-squire test indicate that we reject the null hypothesis. The computed statistic (14.71) is greater than the critical value (7.841).The results indicate that more experienced entrepreneurs have a low tendency toward innovation. The most innovative entrepreneurs are those with 2-5 years of experience. Entrepreneurs with less than two years of experience (50%) show a tendency towards low innovativeness. It is interesting to inquire into the causes of low innovation and low risk-taking by experienced entrepreneurs. Taken together the results indicate a low inclination toward innovation by all entrepreneurs irrespective of experience.

(c) Ho: There is no difference between the level of experience and the concern for greater knowledge of results by entrepreneurs.

The chi-square test indicates that we reject the null hypothesis. The computed X^2 statistic is 13.83. This exceeds the critical value (7.841). The results suggest that there is a high correlation between years of experience and the desire for knowledge of results. More experienced entrepreneurs are more concerned about results of their ventures compared to less experienced entrepreneurs. In general, 69 percent of the firms showed concern about knowledge of results while only 31 percent did not.

(d) Ho: There is no difference between the level of experience and the degree of responsibility of the entrepreneurs.

The results of the chi-square test show that we reject the null hypothesis. We find that the computed X^2 statistic (14.11) far exceeds the critical value (7.814).The results further indicate that more experienced entrepreneurs show higher degree of responsibility than inexperienced ones. In general, 42 percent and 29 percent of entrepreneurs more experienced and less experienced show a high degree of responsibility, whereas 18 percent and 14 percent of entrepreneurs more experienced and less experienced, respectively, show low responsibility.

In summary, experience influences the behaviour of the entrepreneur fundamentally. Specifically, more experienced entrepreneurs show low risk-taking, low innovativeness, high knowledge of results and high responsibility.

(g) Access to credit and entrepreneurial Behaviour

The focus in this section is the impact of the entrepreneur's behaviour on accessing credit for business development. In particular, we examine the relationship between risk-taking and innovative behaviour of entrepreneurs and their access to credit. We formulated and tested the hypotheses below using the chi-square test. All null hypotheses were rejected.

(a) Ho: There is no difference between access to credit and the risk-taking behaviour of the entrepreneurs

The computed X2 statistic (99.76) exceeds the critical value (3.841). Hence we rejected the null hypothesis. The results indicate that 3 percent and 37 percent of entrepreneurs who access and do not access credit respectively are high-risk takers; whereas 4 percent and 56 percent of entrepreneurs, who access and do not access credit, respectively, are low risk takers. In general, there is very low access to credit since only 7 percent of entrepreneurs have access to credit.

(b) Ho: There is no difference between access to credit and the tendency toward innovativeness of the entrepreneurs.

The null hypothesis is rejected when the chi-square test is applied. Specifically, the computed X^2 statistic (101.36) exceeds the critical value (3.841) at 95% confidence interval.

(h) Achievement, Motivation and Entrepreneurial Behaviour

In this section we examine the relationship between achievement motivation and the following behavioural characteristics of entrepreneurs: (a) risk-taking, (b) innovativeness, (c) knowledge of results and (d) sense of responsibility. We formulated and tested the hypothesis below using the chi-square test. The results are reported accordingly. In brief, we rejected all the null hypotheses of independence between achievement motivation and entrepreneurial behaviour above.

(a) Ho: There is no difference between the level of achievement motivation and the risk-taking behaviour of the entrepreneurs.

The computed X^2 statistic (20.97) exceeds the critical value (3.841). Therefore, we rejected the null hypothesis. One further interesting finding here is the fact that low achievement motivation is strongly related to low risk-taking. However, the converse is not true.

(b) Ho: There is no difference between achievement motivation and the level of innovativeness of the entrepreneurs

The results indicate that we reject the null hypothesis. The computed X^2 statistic (22.31) exceeds the critical value (3.841).We also observed a high correlation between low achievement motivation and low inclination towards innovation. The converse case is not implied by the results.

(c) Ho: There is no difference between achievement motivation and the concern with knowledge of results of the entrepreneurs.

Applying the chi-square test to the data, we rejected the null hypothesis. The reason is that the computed X^2 statistic (21.97) exceeds the critical value (2.841).Therefore; achievement motivation determines the knowledge of results. One interesting finding here is that even low achievers have a high knowledge of results. A natural question here is how we rationalize this finding. To answer this question we need to examine the null hypothesis below.

(d) Ho: There is no difference between achievement motivation and the sense of responsibility of the entrepreneurs.

The computerX^2statistic (21.03) exceeds the critical value (0.841). we concluded that achievement motivation influences the sense of responsibility of the entrepreneur. We also found that entrepreneurs with low achievement motivation had a high sense of responsibility. This finding helped us to explain the above result, that entrepreneurs with low achievement motivation have a high knowledge of results.

We inquired further into the relationship between the tendency toward innovation and the level of risk-taking. Our results showed that the two behaviours are not independent of one another. However, the interdependence is a different one, low innovators are low risk takers without implying the converse relation.

In summary, we found a strong relationship between the level of education, training, experience, access to credit, achievement motivation and entrepreneurial behaviour-risk-taking, innovativeness, knowledge of results and responsibility. However, these relationships are asymmetrical. For instance, we found that low innovators are low risk takers, without implying the converse relationships.

(i) Education and Entrepreneurial Behaviour

In order to examine the relationship between education, training, experience, access to credit, achievement motivation and entrepreneurial behaviour we formulated and tested the following hypotheses. We used the

X^2 test in each case and rejected all the null hypotheses of independence. In addition, we regressed entrepreneurial behaviour variables against other possible determinants. The results of the F-statistic, the t-statistic and the value of R^2 were noted and summarized at the end of this section. The results are presented below.

(a) Ho: There is no difference between the level of risk-taking and the level of education of the entrepreneurs.

The computed X^2-statistic was 31.01. When we compared the computed value to the critical value (X^2=7.814) (3df) at 95% confidence interval, we rejected the null hypothesis. Therefore, the level of education of an entrepreneur influences the amount and type of risk undertaken. The results indicated that the 40 percent (53) of the entrepreneurs with high level of education (secondary education and above) were high-risk takers while the majority (60 percent) were low risk takers. Among those with primary level of education, half of them had primary level of education, half of them high-risk takers and the remaining half were low risk takers. Thus, education improves an entrepreneur's sensitivity to and choice of risks. Educated entrepreneurs are risk averse. We also regressed the risk-taking variable against the formal education variable and obtained the results below:

$$R=0.003 + 0.023 \text{ ED}$$
$$(2.673)$$

Where R is the risk-taking behaviour and ED is the level of education of the entrepreneur. The value in the brackets indicates the t-statistic, which is significant at 132 degrees of freedom. Therefore; education strongly influences the risk-taking behaviour of the entrepreneur.

(b) Ho: There is no difference between the level of innovativeness and the level of education of the entrepreneurs.

The computed X^2 statistic was 28.34. When we compared this to the critical value (of 7.814) (3df), we rejected the null hypothesis. The level of education is a determinant of the innovativeness of the entrepreneur. In particular, only 32 percent of the entrepreneurs with high level of education had a high inclination towards innovation. However, 68 percent of the entrepreneurs with a high level of education had a low inclination toward innovation. The entrepreneurs with a low level of education were evenly distributed between low and high inclination toward innovation. A possible explanation for these results is that innovation is expensive.

Since many SMEs do not have access to credit, their aspirations to innovate are dampened.

We also regressed the innovativeness variable against the formal education variable and obtained the results shown below:

$$I = 0.014 \qquad + 0.037 \ ED$$
$$(3.123)$$

Where I is the variable for innovative behaviour and ED is the level of education of the entrepreneur. The value in the brackets indicates the t-statistic, which is significant at 132 degrees of freedom. Therefore, education strongly influences the innovative behaviour of the entrepreneur.

(c) Ho: There is no difference between the level of education and concern for knowledge of results by the entrepreneurs

This hypothesis was not supported by data. We found the computed X^2 statistic (32.81) to be greater than the critical value (7.814).The results demonstrated that entrepreneurs with a high level of education tend to be more concerned about the results of their ventures than those with low or no education. Over 45 percent (69%) of entrepreneurs with high level of education showed high concern for knowledge of results. There is no difference among entrepreneurs with low or no formal education concerning the results of their business activities.

We also regressed the concern for results variable (K) against the formal education variable and obtained the results shown below:

$$K = 0.017 \qquad + 0.009 \ ED$$
$$(3.582)$$

The value in the brackets indicates the t-statistic, which is significant at 132 degrees of freedom. Therefore; education strongly influences the result seeking behaviour of the entrepreneur.

(d) Ho: There is no difference between the level of education and the sense of responsibility of the entrepreneurs

The computed X^2 statistic was 32.43. When compared to the critical value of 7.814, we rejected the null hypothesis. The results indicate that entrepreneurs with a high level of education show a high sense of responsibility compared to those with a low level of education. On the whole, 68 percent of the entrepreneurs with a high level of education demonstrated a high sense of responsibility. For entrepreneurs with a low level of education, 50 percent had a high sense of responsibility and the rest a low sense of responsibility.

We regressed the variable for individual responsibility (RE) against the formal education variable and obtained the results shown below:

$$RE = 0.010 + 0.037 \; ED$$
$$(3.451)$$

The value in the brackets indicates the t-statistic, which is significant at 132 degrees of freedom. Therefore; education strongly influences the entrepreneur's sense of responsibility.

In summary, the level of education influences significantly the behaviour of an entrepreneur. Evidence suggests that the level education determines the level and types of risks taken; the level of innovation, concern about knowledge of results and the sense of responsibility. In particular there is a strong relationship between an entrepreneur's level of education and matters like selling strategy, formation of new ventures, keeping financial records, accountability, and delegation. Entrepreneurs with high level of education show a greater tendency toward record keeping, delegation of duty and an appropriate selling strategy.

(j) Training and Entrepreneurial Behaviour

We formulated and tested the following five hypotheses in order to study the impact of training on the behaviour of the entrepreneur. We applied a chi-square test at 95% confidence interval on all hypotheses. We applied regression analysis on the relevant variables to test the significance of the relationships between them using t-statistics. The results are presented below.

(a) Ho: there is no difference between the level of training and the entrepreneurs concern for knowledge of results

The computed X2 statistic was 21.19 against the critical value of 3.841(1df).Therefore, we rejected the null hypothesis. The results further showed that 69 percent of trained entrepreneurs had a high concern for knowledge of results and only 31 percent had a low concern for results. Among entrepreneurs with no training (39percent of the respondents), 27% had a high concern for knowledge of results; the remaining 12% did not.

We also regressed the risk-taking variable against the variable for training (T) and obtained the results shown below:

$$R = 0.003 \quad + 0.022\ T$$
$$(2.633)$$

Where R is the risk-taking behaviour and T is the level of training of the entrepreneur. The value in the brackets indicates the t-statistic, which is significant at 132 degrees of freedom. Therefore; training also strongly influences the risk-taking behaviour of the entrepreneur.

(b) Ho: There is no difference between the level of training and the level of innovativeness of the entrepreneurs.

We tested hypothesis with a computed X^2 static of 20.96 against the critical value of 3.841. Therefore, we rejected the null hypothesis. While the percentage of entrepreneurs with training who showed greater interest in innovation (20%) was higher than those entrepreneurs without training (13%), the proportion of those who had low interest in innovation was higher (42%) for trained and non-trained (27%) entrepreneurs. Thus, training seems to have little impact of innovation or the tendency to innovate. A possible reason could be lack of capital as a consequence of inaccessible credit.

We also regressed the innovativeness variable against the variable for training and obtained the results shown below:

$$I = 0.013 \quad + 0.032\ T$$
$$(3.571)$$

Where I is the variable for innovative behaviour and T is the level of training of the entrepreneur. The value in the brackets indicates the t-statistic, which is significant at 132 degrees of freedom. Therefore, training strongly influences the innovative behaviour of the entrepreneur.

(c) Ho: There is no difference between the level of training and the tendency toward risk-taking behaviour of entrepreneurs.

The computed X^2 statistic was 23.17. This exceeds the critical value of 3.841. Therefore, we rejected the null hypothesis. Further analysis of the results indicated that 37 percent of entrepreneurs (those with training) showed a low tendency towards risk-taking compared to 24 percent (those with no trained) who showed a high tendency towards risk-taking.

This suggests that training reduces the entrepreneur's tendency towards risk-taking. On the other hand, 16 percent of entrepreneurs sampled (those without training) showed a high tendency toward risk-taking compared to 23 pendent of the entrepreneurs without training and who showed a low tendency towards risk-taking. Taken together, these results support the assertion that entrepreneurs are risk averse, contrary to popular notion that they are risk- seekers.

We also regressed the concern for results variable (K) against the variable for training and obtained the results shown below:

$$K=0.019 \qquad +0.011 \text{ T}$$
$$(3.965)$$

The value in the brackets indicates the t-statistic, which is significant at 132 degrees of freedom. Therefore; training strongly influences the result seeking behaviour of the entrepreneur.

(d) Ho: There is no difference between the level of training and the level of concern with knowledge of results of the entrepreneurs.

Using the X^2 test, we obtained a computed statistic of 24.63 against the critical value of 3.841. The null hypothesis was rejected. The results indicated that 54 percent and 35 percent of entrepreneurs, trained and not trained, respectively, showed low concern for Knowledge of results. This means that training increases the entrepreneurs concern for results from the business.

We regressed the variable for individual responsibility (RE) against the variable for training and obtained the results shown below:

$$RE = 0.010 \qquad + 0.041 \text{ T}$$
$$(4.619)$$

The value in the brackets indicates the t-statistic, which is significant at 132 degrees of freedom. Therefore; training strongly influences the entrepreneur's sense of responsibility.

(e) Ho: There is no difference between level of training and the tendency toward greater responsibility of the entrepreneurs.

The computed X^2 statistic is 23.36. This exceeds the critical value of 3.841 (1df). Therefore we rejected the null hypothesis. The results suggest that training improves the entrepreneur's tendency toward greater responsibility. Indeed, 42 percent and 27 percent of entrepreneurs, trained and untrained respectively, showed a high degree of responsibility.

However, 20 percent and 13 percent of entrepreneurs, trained and untrained, respectively demonstrated a low degree of responsibility.

(k) *Experiences and Entrepreneurial Behaviour*

This section examines the impact of an entrepreneur. We formulated and tested the hypotheses below using the chi-square test at 95 percent confidence interval. We rejected all the null hypotheses. Regression results are also presented below.

(a) Ho: There is no difference between the level of experience and the level of risk-taking of the entrepreneurs.

The computed X^2 static is 12.615. This exceeds the critical value of 7.814 (3 df).Therefore, we rejected the null hypothesis. The results indicated that more experienced entrepreneurs (with 8 years and above) and newly created ventures (<2years) have a low tendency toward high risk-taking behaviour. Only 24percent of all entrepreneurs fell in the above category, whereas entrepreneurs between 2-7 years of experience constituted 36 percent of all respondents. On the other hand, only 16 percent of entrepreneurs with 8 and above years of experience or less than 2 years of experience had a low tendency toward risk-taking; whereas 24 percent consists of entrepreneurs with 2-7 years of experience had a high tendency toward risk-taking. Overall, these results seem to suggest that entrepreneurs are risk seekers. All entrepreneurs, irrespective of years of experience, tend toward high risk than low risk ventures.

We also regressed the risk-taking variable against the variable for experience (E) and obtained the results shown below:

$$R=0.005 \quad +0.025 \ E$$
$$(3.116)$$

Where R is the risk-taking behaviour and E is the level of experience of the entrepreneur. The value in the brackets indicates the t-statistic, which is significant at 132 degrees of freedom. Therefore; experience also strongly influences the risk-taking behaviour of the entrepreneur.

(b) Ho: There is no difference between the level of experience and the tendency toward innovative of the entrepreneurs.

The results of the chi-square test indicated that we reject the null hypothesis. The computed statistic (14.71) was greater than the critical value (7.841).The results indicated that more experience entrepreneurs have a low tendency toward innovation. The most innovative entrepreneurs are those with 2-5 years of experience. Entrepreneurs with less than two years of experience (50%) showed a tendency toward low innovation and low risk-taking by the experienced entrepreneurs. Taken together, the results indicate a low inclination toward innovation by all entrepreneurs irrespective of experience.

We also regressed the innovation variable against the variable for experience and obtained the results shown below:

$$I = 0.03 \qquad +0.107 \ E$$
$$(0.356)$$

Where I is the variable for innovation behaviour and E is the level of experience of the entrepreneur. The value in the brackets indicates the t-statistic, which is significant at 132 degrees of freedom. Therefore, experience does not strongly influence the innovative behaviour of the entrepreneur.

(c) Ho: There is no difference between the level of experience and the concern for greater knowledge of results by entrepreneurs.

The chi-squire test indicated that we reject the null hypothesis. The computed X^2 statistic is 13.83. This exceeds the critical value (7.841). the results suggest that there is a high correlation between years of experience and the desire for knowledge of results. More experienced entrepreneurs are more concerned about results of their ventures compared to less experienced entrepreneurs. In general, 69 percent of the firms showed concern about knowledge of results while only 31 percent did not.

We also regressed the concern for results variable (K) against the variable for experience and obtained the results shown below:

$$K = 0.025 \qquad + 0.214 \ E$$
$$(4.923)$$

The value in the brackets indicates the t-statistic, which is significant at 132 degrees of freedom. Therefore; experience strongly influences the result seeking behaviour of the entrepreneur.

(d) Ho: There is difference between the level of experience and the degree of responsibility of the entrepreneurs

The results of the chi- square test showed that we reject the null hypothesis. We found that the computed X^2 statistic (14.11) far exceeded the critical value (7.814).The results further indicated that more experienced entrepreneurs show higher degree of responsibility than inexperienced ones. In general, 42 percent and 29 percent of entrepreneurs more experienced and less experienced, respectively, showed a high degree of responsibility, whereas 18 percent and 14 percent of entrepreneurs, more experienced and less experienced, respectively, showed low responsibility.

We regressed the variable for individual responsibility (RE) against the experience variable and obtained the suits shown below:

$$RE = 0.017 \quad + 0.134\ E$$
$$(4.824)$$

The value in the brackets indicated the t-statistic, which is significant at 132 degrees of freedom. Therefore; experience strongly influences the entrepreneur's sense of responsibility.

In summary, experience influences the behaviour of the entrepreneur fundamentally. Specifically, more experienced entrepreneurs show low risk-taking, low innovativeness, high knowledge of results and high responsibility.

(l) Access to Credit and Entrepreneurial Behaviour

The focus here is on the impact of the entrepreneur's behaviour on accessing credit for business development. In particular, we examined the relationship between risk-taking and innovative behaviour of the entrepreneurs and their access to credit. We formulated and tested the hypotheses below using the chi-square test. All null hypotheses are rejected. The results of regression analysis are also presented below.

(a) Ho: There is no difference between access to credit and the risk- taking behaviour of the entrepreneurs

The computed X^2 statistic (99.76) exceeds the critical value (3.841). Hence we rejected the null hypothesis. The results indicated that 3 percent and 37 percent of entrepreneurs, who access and do not access credit, respectively, were high-risk takers; whereas 4 percent and 56 percent of entrepreneurs, who access and do not access credit, respectively, were low risk takers. In general, there is very low access to credit since only 7 percent of entrepreneurs have access to credit.

We also regressed the risk-taking variable against the variable for access to credit (AC) and obtained the results shown below.

R= 0.001   +   0.001 AC
                        (2.946)

Where R is the risk-taking behaviour and AC is the access to credit of the entrepreneur. The value in the brackets indicates the t-statistic, which is significant at 132 degrees of freedom. Therefore, access to credit strongly influences the risk-taking behaviour of the entrepreneur.

(b) Ho: There is no difference between access to credit and the tendency towards innovativeness of the entrepreneurs.

The null hypothesis is rejected when the chi-square test is applied. Specifically, the computed X2 statistic (101.36) exceeded the critical value (3.841) at 95% confidence interval.

We also regressed the innovativeness variable against the variable for access to credit and obtained the results shown below:

I = 0.051   + 0.145 AC
                        (4.046)

Where I is the variable for innovative behaviour and AC is the access to credit of the entrepreneur. The value in the brackets indicates the statistic, which is significant at 132 degrees of freedom. Therefore, access to credit strongly influences the innovative behaviour of the entrepreneur.

(m) Achievement Motivation and Entrepreneurial Behaviour

In this section, we examine the relationship between achievement motivation and the following behavioural characteristics of entrepreneurs: Risk-taking, innovativeness, knowledge of results and the sense of responsibility. We formulated and tested the hypothesis below using the chi-square test. The results are reported accordingly. In brief, we rejected all the null hypotheses of independence between achievement motivation and entrepreneurial behaviour above. The regression results are also discussed below.

(a) Ho: There is no difference between the level of achievement motivation and the risk-taking of the entrepreneurs.

The computed X^2 statistic (20.97) exceeded the critical value (3.841). Therefore, we reject the null hypothesis. One further interesting finding here was the fact that low achievement motivation is strongly related to low risk-taking. However, the converse is not true.

We also regressed the risk-taking variable against the variable for achievement motivation (AM) and obtained the results shown below:

$$R = 0.029 \quad + 0.271 \text{ AM}$$
$$(4.617)$$

Where R is the risk-taking behaviour and AM is the achievement motivation of the entrepreneur. The value in the brackets indicates the t-statistic, which is significant at 132 degrees of freedom. Therefore, achievement motivation strongly influences the risk-taking behaviour of the entrepreneur.

(b) Ho: There is no difference between achievement motivation and the level of innovativeness of the entrepreneurs

The results indicated that we reject the null hypothesis. The computed X^2 statistic (22.31) exceeded the critical value (3.841). We also observed a high correlation between low achievement motivation and low inclination towards innovation. The converse case is not implied by the results.

We also regressed the innovativeness variable against the variable for achieving motivation and obtained the results shown below:

$$I = 0.095 \quad + 0.151 \text{ AM}$$
$$(4.939)$$

Where I is the variable for innovative behaviour and AM is the achievement motivation of the entrepreneur. The value in the brackets indicates the t-statistic, which is significant at 132 degrees of freedom. Therefore, achievement motivation strongly influences the innovative behaviour of the entrepreneur.

(c) Ho: There is no difference between achieving motivation and the concern with knowledge of results of the entrepreneurs

Applying the chi-square test to the data, we rejected the null hypothesis. The reason was that the computed X^2 statistic (21.97) exceeded the critical value (2.841). Thus; achievement motivation determines the knowledge of results. One interesting finding here is that even low achievers have a high knowledge of results. A natural question here is how we rationalize this finding. To answer this question, we need to examine the null hypothesis is below.

We also regressed the concern for results variable (K) against the variable for achievement motivation and obtained the results shown below:

$$K = 0.103 \qquad +0.323 \text{ AM}$$
$$(4.432)$$

The value in the brackets indicates the t-statistic, which is significant at 132 degrees of freedom. Therefore; achievement motivation strongly influences the result seeking behaviour of the entrepreneur.

(d) Ho: There is no difference between achievement motivation and the sense of responsibility of the entrepreneurs.

The computed X^2 statistic (21.03) exceeded the critical value (0.841). We concluded that achievement motivation influences the sense of responsibility of the entrepreneur. We also found that entrepreneurs with low achievement motivation had a high sense of responsibility. This finding helped us to explain the above result, that entrepreneurs with low achievement motivation have a high knowledge of results.

We inquired further into the relationship between the tendency toward innovation and the level of risk-taking. Our results showed that the two behaviours are not independent of one another. However, the independence is a different one, low innovators are low risk takers without implying the converse relation.

We regressed the variable for individual responsibility (RE) against the achievement motivation variable (AM) and obtained the results shown below:

$$RE = 0.019 \qquad + 0.257 \text{ AM}$$
$$(4.025)$$

The value in the brackets indicates the t-statistic, which is significant at 132 degrees of freedom. Therefore; achievement motivation strongly influences the entrepreneur's sense of responsibility.

In addition to the above analysis we regressed all the independent variables above against each dependent variable. The results are presented in the table below. The results of the F-test are significant at both 5% and 1% level the coefficients of determination are above 0.5,indicating that education, training, experience, access to credit and achievement motivation are highly correlated with entrepreneurial behaviour.

In summary, we found a strong relationship between level of education, training, experience, access to credit, achievement motivation and entrepreneurial behaviour – risk-taking, innovativeness, knowledge of results and responsibility. However, these relationships are asymmetrical. For instance, we found that low innovators are low risk takers, without implying the converse relationships.

Table 10: Summary of Regression Analysis Results

Independent Variables	Risk - Taking	Innovativeness	Concern For Results	Sense of Responsibility
Education	0.023 (2.673)	0.037 (3.123)	0.009 (3.582)	0.037 (3.451)
Training	0.022 (2.633)	0.032 (3.571)	0.011 (3.965)	0.041 (4.619)
Experience	0.025 (3.116)	0.107 (0.356)	0.214 (4.923)	0.134 (4.824)
Access to credit	0.001 (2.946)	0.145 (4.046)		
Motivation	0.271 (4.617)	0.151 (4.939)	0.323 (4.432)	0.257 (4.025)
F - statistic	3.732	4.156	2.984	4.312
R-square	0.56	0.67	0.63	0.64

3.5 Conclusions

The results of this study indicate that the key factor determining entrepreneurial behaviour among MSEs in Kenya is the need to supplement income. The greatest constraint to Kenyan entrepreneurs is unavailability of credit. While the main strategy employed by MSEs is credit sales, we have argued here that such behaviour reflects the harsh economic environment within which the MSEs are operating in Kenya. We have further contended that if entrepreneurs were offered good jobs that guarantee them a good income which assures them comfort, many of them will abandon their current ventures. The results of this study bare that fact well. This is a confirmation of the fear that there is no (strong) entrepreneurship culture among MSEs in Kenya. However, the study also confirms that the unique characteristic of entrepreneurship is innovation-which we found conspicuously absent among MSEs in Kenya.

In developing countries, constraints to MSEs have been researched and emphasized. We propose that the way forward is for the government to support entrepreneurial development initiatives and programmes amongst micro and small enterprises.

CHAPTER FOUR

DISCUSSION AND CONCLUSION

4.0 Introduction

The factor analysis results presented in the previous Chapter (4) were quantitatively significant in prediction of risk-taking. This was in agreement with the findings advanced by coulter 2000, Mc Clelland (1961) and Drucker (1985).This was precipitated by motivation attitude as a core contributory to entrepreneurial behaviour pattern. It was found however that motivation factor did not influence a lot on predicting innovativeness, individual responsibilities and knowledge of the results from the population of the sample surveyed in the project. The common motives were identified from the research including: innovativeness, risk-taking, individual responsibilities, knowledge or results and experience. The entrepreneurs in this study were influenced at least by their desire and experience to start an enterprise, create employment and wealth characteristics we found to be consistent with their motives of starting micro and small enterprises MSEs. The factors that did not influence entrepreneurial behaviour was found to be retrenchment, desire for being own manager (independence), failure to secure jobs and the desire to generate wealth. This is supported by the notion that business is more profitable, rewarding and challenging.

In the sample surveyed, of Kenyans in business was a safe landing from a frustrating economy which had come with harsh condition after liberalization and hence driving entrepreneurial behaviour amongst micro and small entrepreneurs surveyed.

However the levels of formal education did not have a higher significant influence in the entrepreneurial behaviour tested. We found out that some successful entrepreneurs could not sign their complete name in the legible terms yet they control huge amount of resources both financial, materials and physical. It was an interesting revelation that many entrepreneurs (respondents) were motivated to join business after dropping from formal education for either lack of fees or opportunity. This deterrent precipitated their response to business, as they could not secure a "white collar job' for lack of advanced and formal qualification. It is presenting a strong position that formal education did not influence entrepreneurial behaviours in Kenya although an educated entrepreneur has a high skill and enhanced capacity to approach issues decisions quantitatively and analytically.

From the foregoing discussion, it is apparently clear that formal education is not a determinant of entrepreneurial behaviour which were considered risk-taking, for example innovativeness, individual responsibility and knowledge of results.

The findings suggest that even the lowest echelon of entrepreneurs, who could operate anywhere outside the boundaries of the formal environment in developed countries are subjected to the highest level of bureaucracy, inspections and penalizations. This is a major impediment to growth in the business. Empirical evidence from the result demonstrate regulatory problems especially and practically taxation as among the most severe obstacles to the entrepreneurs. Entrepreneurial firms, MSEs, MFIs were found to be more vulnerable to a high degree of regulatory enforcement. Example is the introduction of "Electronic Tax Register" ETR by ministry of finance administered through the tax administration.

Incidences of bribery, appeared in conjunction with regulatory inspections, whereby bureaucrats utilized this opportunity to exploit, harass entrepreneurs, instead of offering valuable and legitimate services. Cited in this example are the city council, water and electricity departments. However it was learnt that certain characteristics, fast growing firms appear to attract the attention of the council officials to seek bribery and extortion than the slow growth service industry. There was a problem to access public goods and services that facilitate enterprise growth and survival in other countries. There is no safe working environment and lack of effective legal system to address, redress and litigation.

It is suggested in this study that significant reform to be implemented to reduce regulation and regulatory enforcement and it calls for a design of attractive incentives, high standards of accountability for the regulatory and supervisory institutions, to provide for an enabling working environment for micro and small enterprises MSEs. The remedy to this problem will be addressed satisfactorily with the design of policies and programs aimed at mitigation existing regulatory constraints A wide array of constraints faced by MSEs has been discussed at length in this report.

It is apparent that the problems related to access to credit and high cost of doing business are the two most significant ones. Retrenchment and working space are some of the most of the other problems that have adverse effects and micro and small enterprises development in Kenya.

4.1 Challenges Facing MSEs

The research findings revealed that in Kenya today the micro and small enterprises faced many challenges which affected their operations. The most critical challenges faced were:

1. Selling the product/service

Product/service branding

	Frequency	Percent	Valid percent	Cumulative percent
Valid Very much	31	23.3	72.1	72.1
Not much	11	8.3	25.6	97.7
Rarely	1	.8	2.3	100.0
Total	43	32.3	100.0	
Missing System	90	67.7		
Total	133	100.0		

2. Transportation constraints 12.8%

Transport constraints

	Frequency	Percent	Valid percent	Cumulative percent
Valid Yes	17	12.8	100.0	100.0
Missing System	116	87.2		
Total	133	100.0		

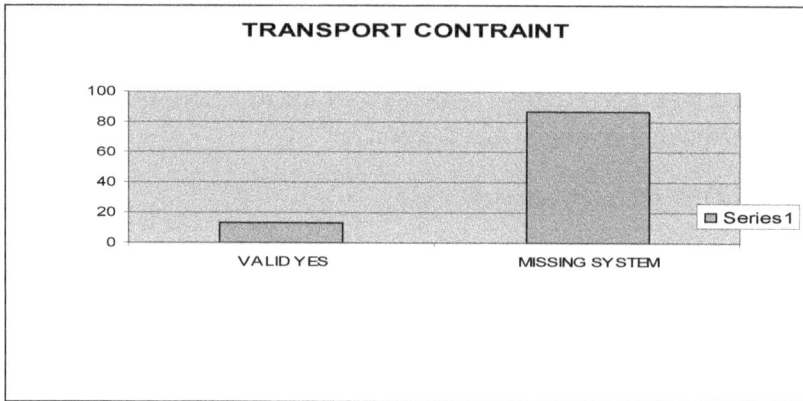

3. Communication (Roads and telephone) 7.5%

Communication (Road and telephone)

	Frequency	Percent	Valid Percent	Cumulative percent
Valid yes	10	7.5	100.0	100.0
Missing system	123	92.5		
Total	133	100.0		

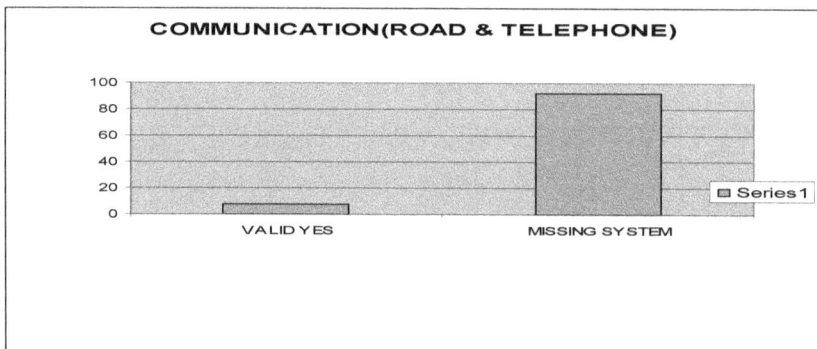

4. Access to (credit) facility 66.2%

Access to loan (credit) facility

	Frequency	Percent	Valid percent	Cumulative percent
Valid Yes	88	66.2	100.0	100.0
Missing System	45	33.8		
Total	133	100.0		

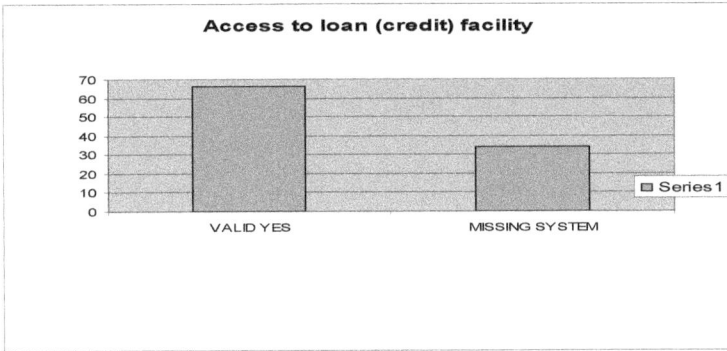

Access to loan (credit) facility

5. *Repayment of loan (credit) 9.8%*

Repayment of loan (credit)

	Frequency	Percent	Valid percent	Cumulative percent
Valid Yes	13	9.8	100.0	100.0
Missing System	120	90.2		
Total	133	100.0		

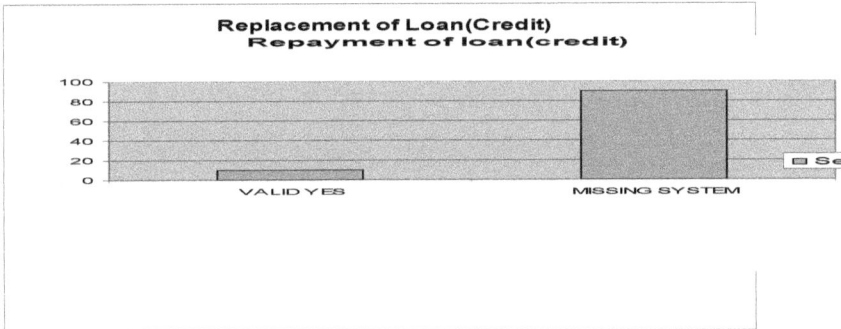

Replacement of Loan(Credit)
Repayment of loan(credit)

6. *Cost of qualified labour 25.6%*

Cost of qualified labour

	Frequency	Percent	Valid percent	Cumulative percent
Valid Yes	34	25.6	100.0	100.0
Missing System	99	74.4		
Total	133	100.0		

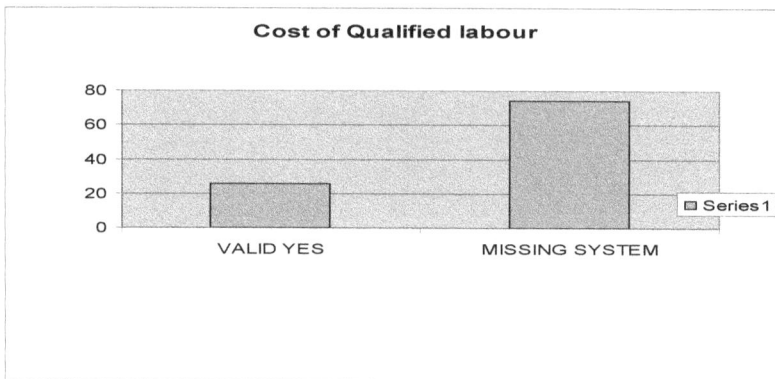

Cost of Qualified labour

7. Formal management discipline 11.3%

Formal management discipline

	Frequency	Percent	Valid percent	Cumulative percent
Valid Yes	15	11.3	100.0	100.0
Missing System	118	88.7		
Total	133	100.0		

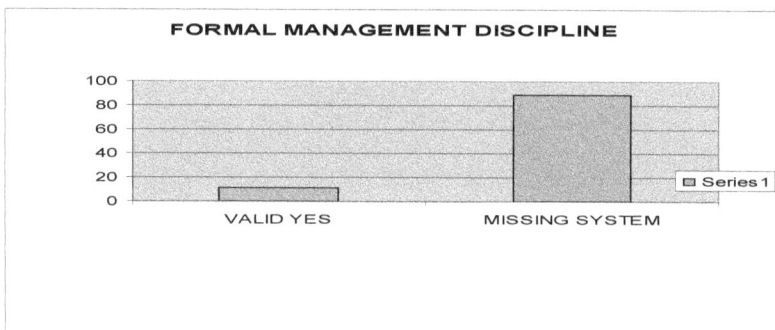

FORMAL MANAGEMENT DISCIPLINE

8. Banking facility 6%

Banking facility

	Frequency	Percent	Valid percent	Cumulative percent
Valid Yes	8	6.0	100.0	100.0
Missing System	125	94.0		
Total	133	100.0		

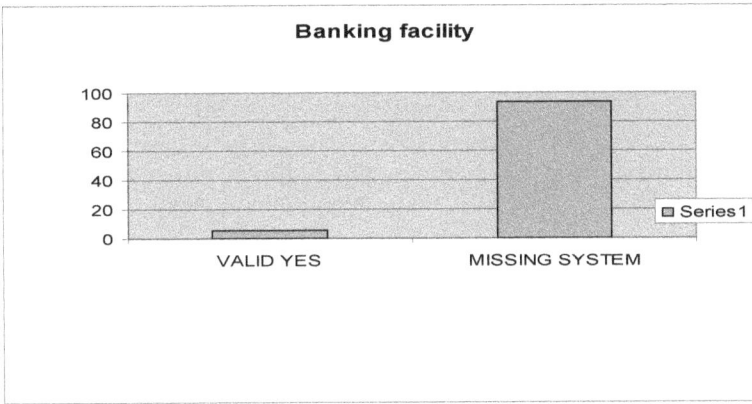

Banking facility

9. *Use of Information Technology (e-mail and Internet) 37.6%*

Use of IT (Email and internet)

	Frequency	Percent	Valid	Cumulative Percent
Valid Yes	5	37.	100.	100.
Missing System	8	62.		
Total	13	100.		

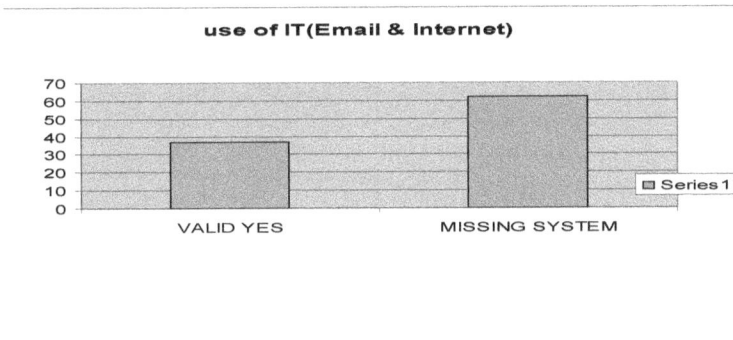

use of IT(Email & Internet)

However it is consoling to talk of the advert of the mobile phones and e-mail facilities which have made possible for the entrepreneur access information with easiness, effectively and efficiently.

The challenges are predominant by mentioned as being common in developing countries. The following are some of the critical challenges daunting many micro and small enterprises in the rest of Africa: Heavy indebtedness, low productivity, weak and inefficient institutional structures, high cost of production, old and obsolete machinery, weak institutional and legal framework, access to affordable credit, poor state of infrastructure, labour turnovers and weak research and extension programmes,(Coulter 2000,Brisa 2001,Drucker 1985,Mc McCormick 1986, Wickham 1998,Schultz 1975,Kinara 2004).

4.2 Recommendations

This study has provided a good forum in presenting the findings by discussing various factors that influence significantly to entrepreneurial behaviour amongst Kenyan Micro and small entrepreneurs. It sought to explain the factors which weigh heavily in terms of significance. It was found that motivation contributed greatly towards influencing a risk-taking innovativeness, knowledge of results and responsibility. It is recommended, therefore that the Government and other agencies and institutions encourage, provide and create an enabling business climate and environment, for the entrepreneurs with high achievement motive to flourish, by giving financial and technical assistance. Indeed this is likely to encourage entrepreneurial behaviour. For example Government sponsored seed capital. It is also agreeing with the entrepreneurial theory as presented in the literature that these factors motivated entrepreneurs amongst MSEs in Kenya to enter into business namely: Desire for independence (self employment), lack of well paying jobs, entrepreneurs desire to make profits and face challenges, retrenchment and downsizing by organization and frustration in a competitive employment in the labour market. From the respondents interviewed the major cause of venturing into business was to seek a solution or substitute for a formal employment that is not available in the Kenyan economy with large trained manpower with huge numbers of unemployment. Formal training according to the survey was a requirement for highly skilled jobs. It was found to have no significance influence in entrepreneurial behaviours which were considered in the survey.

It's agreed with Peter Drucker,(1985),Coulter,(2000) and McCormick,(1986) in their finding and that of various researchers. It is concluded that formal training does not have any bearing with risk-taking and innovativeness on the involvement of the entrepreneur.

However, it is noted that formal training may influence knowledge of results and individual responsibility. It is so because a trained entrepreneur can practice prudent management strategies for example business plans, strategic plans, visionary budget proposal and cash flow statements of any entrepreneurial behaviour amongst the micro small enterprises in Kenya. Experience in previous activities was a great value to influencing entrepreneurial behaviour such as: Innovativeness, risk-taking, knowledge of results and individual responsibility.

Based on the key findings of the research, there are huge and unique challenges facing the small and micro enterprises in Kenya, and the study proposed a number of recommendations to be taken by various government agencies and establishment to stimulate start-up, growth and survival of MSEs, by giving rise to the change of attitude to the stagnated sector. Calling for policy formulation geared towards restructuring of the sector for sustainable growth and renewed governments' commitment, to provide support and impetus for development. Needless to say, within MSEs Framework, the private sector participation, public/private sector partnership and consultations and dialogue is to be considered critical for implementation.

From the research analysis we conducted, it is revealed that 65% of Kenyans economy is driven by micro and small enterprises. However, while it's the case that about 80% of such enterprises will fall by the wayside and 'die along the way' resulting in unemployment situation in the economy and even the effort of wealth creation is hampered.

The findings of this study proposes initiatives and approaches that will realistically sustain the economy and such are driving factors that will be behind economic development. For example the institutional structures that support micro and small enterprises MSEs like Export processing Zone (EPZ),Kenya Industrial Estates (KIE),and Kenya Industrial Research Development (KIRD),to be used to roll out the programmes to remove constraints on the way to rapid progress.

This study proposes the establishment of business incubators. The idea of incubators has proved successful in U.S.A, Japan, Germany, UK, India, and China and is being embraced in South Africa, as a grand plan to remove all obstacles on the way of new start up to growth and survival stage. It is revealed that the concept of incubators is responsible in jump starting the Chinese, Japanese and Indian economies, while it took a lead position in the superior economies in wealth creation. Many industrialized countries of Germany and Sweden have embraced incubators as a strategy to effectively build vibrant and strong economics. It is therefore necessary for micro and small enterprises MSEs in Kenya to produce goods and services capable of competing in the international markets.

By incubators, we mean nurturing, supporting, nourishing and producing new micro and small start-up business by a conducive business climate and enabling environment, until such a time that the

MSEs are able to withstand harsh conditions by sustaining themselves financially with sound managerial practices to stand on their own. The proposed support for the MSEs will range from office space, industrial sites, office facilities (shared), and probably free or subsidized overheads. The findings of this research are that many MSEs are harassed by the local authorities, central government, land owners and other agencies with protection. Other amenities suggested as to benefit the MSEs at start-up are telephones, photocopy, internet facilities that will definitely boost their existence and growth. Technical assistance is a recipe for growth, for example the MSEs will need cash flow statements, books of accounts written for them. Marketing strategies done by incubators to make them functionally self-sustaining. As stated in the research finding MSEs lack vital skills, access to market, capacity to meet cost of doing business, solving venture, start-up problem, we will recommend that the government address challenges in a policy framework, and provide for an enabling business environment. It is evident that, that where implementation has been done, the micro and small enterprises reversed from 30% to 75% success. While studies has revealed that 75% of the MSEs in developing countries, with help of incubators the trend is reversed to 82% success. The notable areas of success are information and communication technology, Agriculture and service industries. The example of China, India and South Africa are Inspirational experiences. Finally we recommend that the Government and other developmental partners shoulder a leading role in supporting the MSEs to eliminate some critical constraints like; registration, taxation, legal and regulatory requirements, office space, internet connection access, computer resources, library and training centre.

Policy Implications

There are definitely several policy implications that emanate from this study. An entrepreneurial behaviour in Kenya to be government supported by enterprising "Kenya" The MSEs will not realize their potential and graduate to competitiveness befitting modern times in terms of quality and quantities, using the appropriate technology, labour and materials. It is worth noting that the government agencies use too much force on MSEs to enforce the legal regulatory framework. For example the government role in micro and small enterprises development is not balanced although we are in a liberalized regime, there is too much "handsoff" management. There should be in place policies that support in a single goal of stakeholdership, to encourage more innovativeness, risk-taking, need for achievement, and pursue opportunities for new markets, for example exports, in profitable business. Indeed such policies should focus towards an enabling small business environment to apply new technologies to improve productivity, search for high potential niche markets, and usage of internet facilities to capture and make use of E-Commerce, E-business to avoid delays in service delivery. Policies on financing and access to credit should be part of the Government annual estimates. It is evident that this sector is hit with lack of credit due to inability by entrepreneurs to provide collateral to the financial institutions, and suggests that the government to put in place flexible but supervised enthusiastic entrepreneurs to commence start up.

Many MSEs Owners are in paid employment and leaving their business to supervisors or hired personnel, who ruin the business by mismanagement. One can argue that they need to gather courage to adapt to full time entrepreneurship if they have to realize full potential and growth in MSEs. It is therefore proposed that entrepreneurs require changing their attitude toward self-employment and taking calculated risks, values and behaviour. Within the entrepreneurs, they need to take advantage of sub-contracting and networking as an exchange of overflowing skills and raw material for example in clustered, Kenyatta market, Gikomba, Kawangware Ngara Market, Kariokor, Ngong Markets and it is proposed that the universities to engage in demand driven research and disseminate such findings to the MSEs for correction improvements of their previous methods of doing business. Similar markets elsewhere in Kenya. The study finding clearly shows that training could significantly contribute to improved performance by micro and small enterprises and other business. The policies in training are lacking and the ones that are available are inadequate to serve the existing entrepreneurs. Indeed there has been joint and concerted effort in training entrepreneurs in universities and colleges in Kenya and abroad, there is a pronounced presence of incubators, seed capital and therefore less effective procedures to encourage risk-taking in as many Kenyan as possible. However, NGO and MFI(s)have registered their presence but yet the demand for training by entrepreneurs is overwhelming. However it is incumbent upon the government to promote policies towards training to foster the development of entrepreneurial characteristics and behaviour while other agencies for example development partners to direct its effort and focus on areas of risk-taking, innovativeness and opportunity marshalling.

Contribution to Knowledge

The study shows that organization and institutions theories contribute effectively to micro and small enterprises. For example Scott, 1975, Olsen 1984 cited how institutions are responsible for providing structures and are sets of constraints that govern the behavioural interactions.

In other words, this study has utilized the literature on organizational, institutional and entrepreneurial behaviour, amongst micro and small enterprises. The MSEs were adopting appropriate institutional and organizational innovativeness and risk-taking opportunities, (Drucker 1985).

It has been established that entrepreneurship in micro and small enterprises is adoptable just as in medium and large companies.

Consequently, it is imperative that micro and small enterprises demand for them to map out the course of their own destiny that will encompass demand driven supply which will lead to better and economical utilization of resources i.e. financial, human and physical resources.

It is concluded that an enabling institutional environment to promote entrepreneurial behaviour for dynamism, innovativeness and entrepreneurial owner-managers instead of imitating entrepreneurs.

Implications to entrepreneurs and other institutions

The study has provided a road map that may be pursued, by those who may be persuaded, by those who may find it in line with their curiosities to practice, adopt to create micro and small enterprises. This is a perfect example of a business incubator.

Similarly, institutions that are MSEs, MFIs and NGOs could use the results to design effective programmes to the benefit of the concerned entrepreneurs. The result proposes a solution to removing the constraints as a conscious design and interaction. (Scott 1987).

4.3 Limitations of Study

It should be noted that micro and small enterprises are not accommodated in the legal and regulatory frameworks and therefore a new phenomenon, although MSEs was introduced in 1972,no specific emphasis or policy has been put in place to support and promote entrepreneurship,40 years after independence from the British Government.

Taxation systems in Kenya has discriminated on the MSEs entrepreneurs so whenever MSEs visited by a researcher they tend to be resistant to offering any credible interview in a research response.

The last limitation is that the data used for generalization was cross-sectional and collected under suspicious environment.However, the results and the findings could be better if such data was longitudinal instead of cross-sectional. It could have resulted in a much realistic findings and generalizations.

The study faced some limitations in the following areas:-

1. The research faced some serious time constraint and as a result only a few variables that influence entrepreneurial behaviour were studied in the factor analysis models. The sample size was small. We suggest that the findings could have portrayed different results if more variables were considered and tested.
2. The research and his assistants found some hostility from the respondent at Kariobangi South light industries (KSLI) who have been frustrated by poor economics and wide spread corruption scandals in the government and did not want to listen to anything directed to policy implementation or information. The respondents were greatly disillusioned about research as they associated it with government services which are wanting, as far as the micro and small enterprises are concerned.
3. Language was some barrier to some respondents in answering the questions, some words could not be easily translated to local languages from English. It was a great determination as some terminologies had no equivalent in Kiswahili, Kikuyu, Luhyia, Dholuo And Ekegusii. The catchments area of Kariobangi South Light Industries (KSLI) has that diversity of many respondents from the mentioned ethics groups, and some words were impossible for us to translate.

4.4 Suggestion for Further Research in MSEs

The finding for this research set a ground for further research for the following areas:

The study was conducted in Nairobi which has well informed businessmen. It is necessary to conduct a similar study in other towns like Mombasa, Nakuru, Thika, Kakamega and Kisii where the results could be compared. This study has encompassed both men and women. A comparative study will bring out the dominant group with entrepreneurial behaviour whether men or women and the precipitating factors other than those tested herein.

A more specific study on family enterprises/ventures and the unique succession plan that is problematic. The study conducted was more on entrepreneurial behaviour.

Time was a major constraint and a limitation to this study. it made it difficult to study a large number of factors (e.g. political, economical, ecological, psychological and geographical)that might contribute to the determination of entrepreneurial behaviour.

Gender disparity as a constraint to entrepreneurship would be a good area for study to explore why more women starting enterprises fail to go through start-up, growth and survival stages in Kenya. By way of replication, similar studies should be considered in other cities or towns to strengthen and affirm the findings of this study and in this case a similar study needs to be conducted in Mombasa, Kisumu, Nakuru, Nyeri and Kisii where a host of entrepreneur is displaying various entrepreneurial behaviour and talents. Great effort has gone into this project to contribute to knowledge in the area of entrepreneurial behaviour; the researcher appreciated and recognizes information gaps, unanswered questions that another scholar should keenly address in further research. These include:

- The role of women entrepreneurs in Kenya
- The role of micro and small enterprises in Kenya.
- Legal and regulatory framework as an impediment to entrepreneurial climate. The case of taxation in Kenya. This has been a thorny issue for MSEs for example to acquire registration, licenses and utilities.
- Factors affecting entrepreneurial growth and development in East African Community (EAC) with specific example to member states: Kenya, Uganda and Tanzania.

QUESTIONNAIRE

PART A: BIO DATA

1. Name of the business..
2. Plot No:..

Respondent's Details
Name (optional)...

3. Position in the business

Proprietor	Other staff
	Position

4. Gender

Male	Female

5. Age

Below 25	26-35	36-45	46-55	Over 56

Tick as appropriate

6. Education

Primary	Secondary	Tertiary	University

7. Period in this type of business

Below Years	2-5 years	5-8 years	8-10 years	Over 10 years

8. Type of MSE

Trade	
Manufacturer	
Construction	
Bar/hotel/restaurant	
Services	

Tick as necessary

9. Number of employees (including proprietors)

1	2	3-5	6-10	More than 10

PART B

Factors that Determine Entrepreneurial Behaviour

10. Which of the following factors motivated you or owner of this business to start the business? Please tick. You may tick more than one.

	Item	Tick as necessary
a)	Encouraging government policy	
b)	The desire to be own boss	
c)	Attraction of a higher income/profits	
d)	Need to supplement income	
e)	Desire to generate wealth	
f)	Existence of demand for the product/ service	
g)	Availability of credit	
h)	Retrenchment	
i)	Failure to secure a job	
j)	Other (please specify).................	

11. If you completed (j) of question 8, please specify ....
....
....

12. On a scale of 1 to 5, please indicate to what extent the following factors compelled you or in your opinion compelled the owner of the business to start up 1 represents least compelling and 5 represents *most compelling.*

	1	2	3	4	5
a) Encouraging government policy					
b) The desire to be own boss					
c) Attraction of a higher income /profit					
d) Need to supplement income					
e) Desire to generate wealth					
f) Demand for product/service					
g)Availability of credit					
h) Retrenchment					
i) Failure to secure a job					
j) Other (specify)..					

13. How do you normally obtain your business? Please tick one.

Bid for tenders	
Through connections	
Look for customers	
Through a pool of loyal customers	
Other (specify)............................	

14. Do you normally use marketing strategy for your products/services?

YES   NO

15. If Yes, which strategies do you use on a scale of 1 to 3 (Very Much, Not Much, Rarely)

Marketing Strategies	Very much	Not much	Rarely
Pricing and use of discounts			
Product/ service branding			
Choice of distribution channels			
Credit sales			
Cash only sales			
Other (please specify).................			

PART C

Dominant Factors

16. Which common challenges do you face in your business? You may choose more than one.

17. On a scale of 1 to 3, indicate toward what extent the following factors are key challenges.

Selling the products/services	
Transportation constraints	
Communication (Road & Telephone)	
Access to loan (credit)	
Cost of qualified labour	
Formal management discipline	
Banking facility	
Use of IT(E-mail and Internet)	
Other (specify).........................	

18. Did you have any training in this type of business before starting up?

Factors	Very Dominant	Not so dominant	Occasionally Dominant
Selling the product/service			
Transportation constraints			
Communication			
Access to loan facilities			
Repayment of loans			
Cost of qualified labour			
Cost of supplies			
Formal management styles			
Banking			
Use of IT			
Others (specify..............			

19. If your answer above is YES, indicate the type of training.

    YES   NO

20. Who manages your business?

Formal (school, college, etc.)	
Apprenticeship	
Experience former employment	
Other (specify).........................	

PART D

Entrepreneurial Culture

21. If you were offered a well-paying job in a formal sector, would you take it?

YES	NO

22. If your answer in question 19 is yes, under what conditions would you accept the job offer?

Would demand no conditions	
Where monthly salary is more than monthly return	
Where offered position of responsibility/management	
Other (specify)...	

23. Do you maintain formal financial records?

YES	NO

24. If your answer above is YES, how often do you analyse your financial records to see how well you are doing?

Daily	
Weekly	
Monthly	
Annually	
Other (specify)	

25. Whom would you normally employ in a management position in your business?

A relative	
Non family member	
A qualified person regardless	
Other (specify)...	

26. Do you normally attend seminars/conferences deliberately meant to improve management of your business?

    YES   NO

27. If your answer above is YES, why? Give reasons for your answer.
    ....
    ....

28. If your answer in question 26 is NO, Why? Give a maximum of 2 reasons
    ....
    ....

29. Do you retain a written business plan? ....
    ... ...
    ....

30. Do you have a written vision or mission statement? ....
    ... ...
    ....

31. Why do you charge the current price(s) for your products or services?
    ....
    ....

32. Are any of the employees you have related to you in any way?

33. Would you prefer formal employment to your business?

34. What is the opinion of your closest friends and relatives about whether you should prefer formal employment to business? ......
    ....
    ....

35. What is, in your opinion, the attitude of most Kenyans to those of you in business/self-employment? ....
    ... ...
    ....

36. Please describe how you would like your business to grow in the next five to ten years. ....
....

PART E

Future / General

37. Have you received any government support in your business?

    YES   NO

38. If your answer in number 37 is yes, which support have you received?
....
....

39. Suggest what the Government should do to enhance your business efforts. ....
....

40. Are you happy with the performance of your business in terms of turnover or profits?

    YES   NO

41. Please give your opinion on the following:

Kenyans prefer to take business risks when they see or are given a chance.

Strongly Agree	Agree	Neutral	Disagree	Strongly Disagree
1	2	3	4	5

b) Given the choice between running own business or employment, majority of Kenyans will prefer running own business.

Strongly Agree	Agree	Neutral	Disagree	Strongly Disagree
1	2	3	4	5

c) The Kenyan business environment supports small enterprises.

Strongly Agree	Agree	Neutral	Disagree	Strongly Disagree
1	2	3	4	5

d) To succeed in my business in future, I will need to use more of internet-mail and ICT (information Communication Technology) in general.

Strongly Agree	Agree	Neutral	Disagree	Strongly Disagree
1	2	3	4	5

Thank you for your time and patience in completing this questionnaire.

FOCUS GROUP DISCUSSION GUIDE

Introduction

My name is Isaac Maragia. I am a PhD student at the department of Business Administration, Washington International University, USA.I am conducting field work research for purposes of writing a thesis. The topic for my study is, "THE FACTORS THAT DETERMINE ENTREPRENEURIAL BEHAVIOUR: A STUDY OF MICRO AND SMALL ENTERPRISES IN KENYA."

I request that I discuss with you some issues affecting your business i.e. factors that motivated you to join business, constraints and support initiatives, for example the infrastructure, security, etc.

I look forward to your support in generating information necessary to compile this report. The findings of my study will be useful to policy makers, implementers and stakeholders in providing solutions to problems faced by micro and small enterprises in Kenya.

I wish to introduce my colleague. Her/his name is_____ she/he is assisting me to collect data. I will give you an opportunity to introduce yourselves. Please tell us your age, religion and what you do. The information you will provide will be treated with confidentiality and will not be used for any purpose, other than my PhD research studies.

It is my request that you discuss freely and openly and ask your questions at the end of the group discussion. Indeed, there are no wrong and right answers and so you are free to express your opinion.

We request to tape record this discussion. We need your permission to do so. At the end of the session, we will give you a chance to listen to what you have said during the discussion.

Questionnaire for Focus Group Discussion Guide

1. What is the type of your business? (Tick the appropriate)
    i.   Service industry oriented   Yes/No ( ) ( )
    ii. Goods and Service industry oriented   Yes/No ( ) ( )
    iii. Manufacturing industry oriented   Yes/No ( ) ( )
    iv. Both Good and Service industry oriented Yes/No ( ) ( )

2. What is your educational background?
    i.   Primary   ( )
    ii.   Secondary   ( )
    iii. Tertiary   ( )
    iv.   Degree   ( )
    v.   Professional   ( )

3. How many years have you been in business?
    (i) 1   ( )   (ii) 2   ( )   (iii) 3   ( )
    iv) 5   ( )   (v) 10   ( )   (vi) 20   ( )

4. Did you have previous experience in business?   Yes ( )   No ( )

5. Are you experiencing some difficulties in your business in the following areas?

    i.   Selling your products / services   Yes   ( )   No   ( )
    ii.   Transport   Yes   ( )   No   ( )
    iii. Communication   Yes   ( )   No   ( )
    iv.   Loan facilities   Yes   ( )   No   ( )
    v.   Overdraft facilities   Yes   ( )   No   ( )
    vi.   Credit facilities   Yes   ( )   No   ( )
    vii. Supplies   Yes   ( )   No   ( )
    viii. Qualified manpower to hire   Yes   ( )   No   ( )
    ix.   Banking facilities   Yes   ( )   No   ( )

6. Did you have formal employment before joining business?
        Yes ( )   No ( )

7. If you were offered a well-paying job in formal sector with an income higher than your turnover/return per month, would you take it?
    Yes ( )   No ( )

8. What was your main reason for starting business?
    i.   Wanted to be independent
    ii.   Retrenchment
    iii. Lack of employment
    iv.   Business is more challenging
    v.   In business one makes more profit
    vi.   Formal employment was frustrating
    vii. Other: specify...

9. Which methods do you apply in distributing goods/services in your business?
   Selling goods or services: Quoted 25% above competitors
   viii. Selling on account (credit)
   ix. Both cash & on account.

10. What action is appropriate for your situation given ....
    ....

11. In procurement procedures, a tender / quotation is floated in the local dailies. It specifies the requirements and fortunately, it falls within the range of the goods/services that you provide, but it is definitely bigger than your financial resources. There is a non-refundable fee of KShs 5,000. What would you do?
    (i) Apply for the tender documents ( ) or
    (ii) Avoid applying to forgo competition and wastage of your money ( )

12. For the time you have operated a business, you have experience growth in profit & sales, manpower and employment. Indeed it has been slow than expected. Which would you do?
    (i) Expand your business?
    (ii) Consolidate, concentrate on the existing structures of your business i.e. products and keep on the rate of growth.

13. You have adopted a given strategy/method in your business for years. Although there has been demand for your products and business kept on growing, you have met these demands. Which would you do?
    i.   Improve and maintain the existing successful production procedures
    ii. Develop new techniques, produce new products or services

14. In the same situation above (14),which would you adopt?
    (i) Hire quality employees
    (ii) Recruit and or train in – house
    (iii) Look and hire better – qualified manpower.

15. From the seminar / conference you attended, you have learned that there is need to minimize the method of production and by-product is a raw material for another product. What would you do?
    (i) Focus your efforts on making a new product
    (ii) See the new product as a new opportunity to innovate and expand the enterprise.

16. Product / service you sell:
    i.   Are they original ?   Yes   ( )   No   ( )
    ii. If the answer to (i) is No, have you modified the product,
         packaging or handling the existing service or product?
         Yes ( )   No   ( )
    iii. Are your selling tactics superior from those used by your
         competitors?   Yes ( ) No ( )
    iv. If the answer to   (iii) is No, are your distributions or selling
         tactics your original idea or copied from your competitor?
         Original idea ( ) Copied from competitor ( )
17. Is this a family business? Yes   ( )   No   ( )

18. Who manages the business?
    i.   Self   ( )
    ii. Wife   ( )
    iii. Family   ( )
    iv. Employees   ( )
    v.   Management   ( )

19. Which of the following may not be done without your approval/
    authority?
    (i)   Accepting return on defective goods
    (ii) Purchasing of stock
    (iii) Selling of products / services
    (iv) Authorizing credit to customers

20. Do you maintain financial records (computerized accounts or
    manuals records)?
               Yes ( )   No ( )

21. If yes to No. 20, how often do you analyse your financial records to
    determine the performance of your business?
    i.   Daily   ( )
    ii. Weekly   ( )
    iii. Monthly   ( )
    iv. Annually   ( )
    v.   Others   ( )

22. Do you prepare a schedule for your business activities?
               Yes ( )   No ( )

23. If yes above, how often do you prepare. Explain.

    i)   Daily   ( )
    ii) Weekly   ( )
    iii) Monthly   ( )
    iv) Annually   ( )

24.

a) Are you happy with the performance of your business?

              Yes ( )   No ( )

b) If your answer above is YES, in what way are you satisfied with the performance of your business?

    i)   Volume of sales has increased
    ii) Turnover increased
    iii) Workforce increased
    iv) Profits increased

c) If your answer to Q. 24 is NO, what are your dissatisfactions to the business performance?

    i)   Decline in sales
    ii) Low profit
    iii) Stiff competition
    iv) Loss of market

BUSINESS PLAN

1. Your business idea...
....

2. What is the name of your business? ....
....

3. What is the competitive advantage of your business? ....
....
....

4. <u>Marketing</u>

• Type of business you are in:

Manufacturer	Wholesaler	Retailer	Services
Wholesaler	Retailer	Consumer	Consumer

• Consumer Description:
   - Describe your target consumer
   - Expected age of your consumer
   - Expected gender of your consumer
   - What will product fulfil   _____
   - Financial status of your consumer   _____

5. <u>Promotion / Advertising</u>
   - How will you reach the consumer?
   - What is the slogan of your business
   - Will you make sales calls   YES   NO
   - Write a presentation for sales
   ----

6. Economics

Service Company:

- Define your units_____
- Selling prices per unit_____ (menu)
- Costs of services sold per unit
- Labour --
- Supplies --
- Labour (work force)
- Entrepreneurial time per hour_____
- How long it takes to complete a job_____
- Labour cost per unit = 2x3 = 6

7. Supplies

- What are the costs of supplies per consumer?
- -------------------------------------
- Costs of services per unit?-
- -------------------------------------
- Gross profit per unit
- ---
- Selling price per unit_____
- Cost of services sold per unit equals gross profit per unit

8. Market Research

Competition

Conduct a survey. Ask two people these questions about your business and record their responses as follows:

a) Do you like the name of my business?
  1. YES ------------------
  2. NO --------------------

b) What do you think of my logo?
  1._____like it
  2. _____ a little confusing

c) Where would you like to go to buy my product?
  1. Come home
  2. I don't like a stranger in my house

d) Do you think my product/service has value?

     1. YES--------------------

     2. YES--------------------

e) How could you improve my business idea?

....

f) How much would you pay for my service/product?

    1._____ KShs 100

    2._____ KShs 150

g) Who are my closest competitors?

....

h) Why is my product/service going to beat the competition?

....

i) Do you think my product/service is better or worse than that offered by my competitor(s)?

          YES   NO

9. Strategy for a business selling

		Door to door	Flea Market	School/ Church function	Street Vendor	Local Store	Your own home	Internet Marketing	Others
SELLING METHODS	Business Cards								
	Posters								
	Flyers								
	Phone								
	Sales calls								
	Brochure								
	Mailings								
	Others								

10. Legal Structure

    (i) Sole proprietorship

    (ii) Partnership

    (iii) Corporation

    (iv) NGO

    (v) Explain your decision......................................

    (vi) Legal fee ....

(vii) What permit/licenses do you need for your business?.............................

(viii) Statutory bodies you need to contact for registration.
1. KRA
2. NSSF
3. Labour
4. NHIF
5. Trade
6. Local authority
7. Professional body
8. NGO Council

11. <u>Start up costs</u>
   • Estimated start-up cost...........................

<u>Item</u>   <u>Where you buy them</u>   <u>Cost</u>

Estimated total start-up cost_____

12. List sources of finance below (in detail):

DESCRIPTION	ATM	EQUITY INVESTMENT	DEBT LOAN	GIFT
Personal savings (SACCO)	100			
Relatives		100		
Friends			100	
Investors				100
Grant			100	
Others				
Total	500			

13 For equal financing, what % of ownership will you give up?_____20%

Debt financing: interest rate you will pay? 10%

Operating cost _____

Monthly fixed cost_____ (includes salaries, utilities, advertising, interest, insurance and rent).

<u>Variable costs</u> (Fluctuate)

Monthly budget (Income statement)
Budgeted yearly income_____statement

- Sales (Total sales)
- Costs (Cost of sales)

Total cost of services sold
- Gross profit
- Fixed expenses
- Variable costs
- Operating costs

<u>Profit</u>

Profit/loss before taxes
Less taxes 25%
Net profit [1]

---

1   Adapted from Steve Mariotti (1996), pp.325 – 348. The Young Entrepreneur's Guide to Starting and Running a Business. Three Rivers Press,
New York, 1996.

BIBLIOGRAPHY

Allen. D. and Syedur Rehman. (1985). *"Small Business Incubators: a Positive Environment for entrepreneurship"* Journal of small Business Management, 1985, pp.12 -21.

Aleke Dando, C. (1995). The changing Roles of Key Institutions in Implementation of Credit programmes for Small Scale Enterprise development in Kenya. In English and Henault (1995)

Audrallt, Epperson. (2002). Tough-minded ways to get innovative enterprises. Harvard Business Review, Aug. 2002, p. 117-124.

Audretsch, D.B. (2002). *Entrepreneurship: A Survey Of The Literature.* Prepared for the European Commission, Enterprise Directorate General 1 institute for Development Strategies, Indiana University & centre for Policy Research (CEPR), London, July 2002.

Bates Timothy and Nucci A. (1989). *"An Analysis of Small Business Size and Rate of Discontinuance,"* Journal of small business management October 1989.

Baumol, W. J. (1989). *Entrepreneurship:: Productive, Unproductive and Destructive.* Journal or Political Economy, 1990 Vol. 98 No.3 pp. 893 – 921, The University of Chicago.

Barley, Sue (1989). *"Female Entrepreneurs: Are they really any different?"* Journal of Small Business Management, January 1989, pp. 32-37.

Bongems, L. (1987). *Technology and Industrialization: A Network Approach.* Dept. of Industrial Management and Economics, Chalmers University of Technology, 41296 Gotenborg – Sweden.

Bricklin, Dan. (2001) *"Natural – Born Entrepreneur",* Harvard Business Review, September 2001, pp. 53 – 58

Burns,P. and J. Dewhurst, ends. (1996) Small Business and Entrepreneurship (2nd Edition), McMillan.

Bulunywa. (1998). Entrepreneurship and Small Business Enterprises growth in Uganda, Makerere University Business School Kampala Uganda.

Bwisa H.M.(2001) *"Promoting demand driven S & T Policy Research for Kenya's Microprocessors"* A concept paper-background paper at National Workshop for Jua Kali Agro-Processors ATPS and IDRC July 2001, NAIROBI.

Bwisa, H. M. ,(2001). Entrepreneurship and Learning, notes by Prof. H. M. Bwisa, University of Nairobi.

Bwisa, H. M. (1998). How to Find and Create a Business Opportunity.

Bwisa, H. M. (1998).Demand Driven MSE(s) Research in Kenya Critical Issues.

Christian Marrisson, Henri- Bernard Solignac Leconite, Xaviern Oudin. (1994). *Micro Enterprises and the Institutional Framework in Developing Countries.* OECD-Publication, Paris Cedex 16 France.

Coulter, K. Mary.(2000). *"Entrepreneurship in Action",* Prentices Upper Saddle River, New Jersey.

Cooper, R. Donald and C.William Emory. (1995). *Business Research Methods.* Irwin, Mc Graw – Hill.

Darrel Rigby and Chris Zook. (2002). *"Open Market innovation",* Harvard Business Review, October 2002, p.81 – 85.

Dorothy McCormick.(1998). *Gender in small enterprises development in Kenya: An Institutional Analysis,* University Of Nairobi.

Douglas Holtz–Eakin. (2000). *Public Policy Toward Entrepreneurship",* Small Business Economics 15:283 -291, 2000 - Netherlands.

Donald Mead. (1993). *"Agents in change in policy development and Implementation for small enterprises"* Sme Conference PME-Abidjan 30th November to 2nd December 1993.

Drucker, P. F. (1998). *"The Disciple of innovation",* Harvard business Review, Nov – Dec 1998, pp. 149 – 157. *the black",* Harvard Business Review, April 2002. pp. 133 -117.

Drucker P.F. (1986). *Innovation and Entrepreneurship, Practice and Principles,* Harper Business, New York, NY 10022. USA.

Drucker, P.F (1985), *Innovation and Entrepreneurship: practice and principles,* Butter worth – Heinemann London U.K.

Drucker, P.F.(1985 pp 125) *"Implementing entrepreneur ideas. The case for intention,"* Vol. 13 No 3 (entrepreneurial intentionally).

Ferrand, D. (1997), *Discontinuity in development:* The Case of Kenya's Missing Middle, University of Durham, UK.

Ferrand, D. V. (1998). Discontinuity in development: Kenya's Middle – Scale- Manufacturing Industry, Thesis for Doctor of Philosophy, University of Dunham.

Garnir, B. and Gasse Yvon. (1990). *"Training entrepreneurs through Newspapers"* Laval University, Quebec journal of Small Business Management, January 1990 pp. 70 – 73.

Gartner, B. William. (1989). *"Who is an entrepreneur? Is the wrong question",* Journal of Entrepreneurship Theory and Practice, summer 1989, University of Baltimore pp. 47 – 68.

Gibb, A. (1999). *"Creating an Entrepreneurial Culture in support of SME(s)",* Journal of Small enterprise Development, Vol. 10, No. 4, 27-28.

Gok/ILO/UNDP (1989). *A Strategy for Small Enterprises Development in Kenya: towards the Year 2000.* A Government of Kenya Report, Nairobi.

Gok, Kepsa. (2003).Ministry of Planning and National Development, proceedings of the National Investment Conference 2003, pp.56 – Micro and Small Enterprises MSE(s).

Gok. (2003). *Interim Investment Programme for the Economic Recovery Strategy for Wealth and Employment Creation 2003 – 2007.*

GoK. (1992). Sessional Paper No. 2 (1992) Government of Kenya Publication, 1992.

GoK. (2004).Sessional Paper No.3 of 2004, *Development of Micro and Small Enterprises for Wealth Creation and Employment Generation.*

GoK. (1999). National MSE Baseline Survey 1999, Central Bureau of Statistical (CBS).

Hayek. (1996). *Perception, Opportunity and Knowledge: A Subjective View of the Role of Information.* Conference material on Austria Economics held at Irving, Texas U.S.A., December 1976.

Hebert F. Robert and Link N. Albert. (1989). *"In search of the meaning of entrepreneurship. The entrepreneur: The catchword or crucial concept?"* Small Business Economics (1989) 39 – 49. Auburn-U.S.A. University of Carolina, U.S.A.

Hirsch, R.D. (1998). *"Entrepreneurship: past, present and future."* Journal of small Business Management, October 1988 pp. 1-4.

Hisrich R.D. and Brush C.(1986), *"Characteristics of the Minority Entrepreneurs,"* Holt David H. (2001). *Entrepreneurship: New Venture Creation.* Prentice Hall of Judia, New Delphi 110001 – 2001.

Hubert Schmitz and Khalid Nadvi. Clustering and Industrialization: Introduction, Institute of development Studies," University of Sussex, UK World Development Vol.27, No.9pp. 1503 – 1514, 1999. Great Britain.

ILO. (1996). *Structural Adjustment and Employment Policy.* Geneva Switzerland.

Jeanne Downing. (1990). *"Gender and the Growth and Dynamics of Micro Enterprises",* Journal of Small Business Management, October 1986, pp. 1 – 8.

Joy O. Robert. (1989). Cultural and procedural Differences that influence Business Strategies and Operations in the People's Republic of China. Sam Advanced Management Journal, Vinton, VA 24179.

Jorgen Bill toft. (1996). *"Between Industrialization: The Dilemma of support for micro activities."* A policy study of Kenya and Bangladesh and income generation.

Jovahovics (1992) Kenneth Loucks (1988). *Training entrepreneurs for small Business creation: Lessons from experience.* ILO publication No. 26 Geneva.

Kibera F.N. (1996). *Introduction to Business: A Kenya Perspective,* Kenya Literature Bureau, Nairobi, Kenya.

Kielen E. Gersick, John A. Davis, McCollon Hampton. (1997). *Generation to generation: Life Cycles of Business Family Business,* Harvard Business School Press, Boston Massachusetts.

Kimani, Elishiba. (2001). *Gender and Economic Recovery.* National Dialogue on Economic Recovery, Collaborative Centre for Gender and Development, Department of Development Studies, Kenyatta University, 2001.

Kinara, E.O. (2004). Ph.D. thesis, "Mobilizing Savings of the poor in addressing their Poverty of Financial Services the case of Kibera Slums, Nairobi."

King, Kenneth and McGrath, S. (1999). *Enterprise in Africa: Between poverty and Growth,* Intermediate Technology Publications, London.

Kinyanjui, M. and Munguti, K. (1997). "Gender Equity" in Micro and Small Enterprises in Kenya.

Kinyanjui, M. N., McCormick, D. and P. Kimuyu. (2001) "Kenya's Garment Industry: An Institutional view of medium and large firms," Paper prepared for presentation at a conference on Business Systems in Africa, IDS, University of Nairobi in collaboration with CDR-Copenhagen.

Kirzner, Israel M. (1979). Perception Opportunity and Profit: Study in the Theory of Entrepreneurship, Chicago: University of Chicago press.

Kirzner. (1992). "The Entrepreneurial Function is to notice what people have overlooked" the theory of Entrepreneurship in Economic Growth, 1982, pp. 273.

Knight, Frank H. (1921). Risk, Uncertainty and Profit, Chicago University of Chicago Press.

Kristler Ahlstrom. (1998). *"Governing the family owned Enterprises,"* Harvard Business Review, Jan - Feb, 1998, p.155 – 123.

Leo, Paul Dana. (1984). International note, Coping with Entrepreneurial Stress: Evidence from Nigeria. Levin, R.I. and Rubin, David S. (2001). Statistics for Management. Prentice Hall, India New Delhi.

Maragia I. M. (2003). *Towards the understanding of Entrepreneurial Behaviour amongst Kenya micro small enterprises.* "Independent Study paper" Doctoral Studies, University of Nairobi (Entrepreneurship and Small Business Development. DSE 703-2003.

Maragia I. M. (1990). *The Accounting Profession: Power and politics in Organization Context.* Prepared for the Doctorate Course: Management and Financial Control – Concepts and methods for an Archaeology of Accounting (5p) University of Lund, Spring 1990.

Mead, Donald. (1993). *The way in which Legal Regulatory and Tax Framework affects the Dynamics of Enterprises growth.* Department of Economics, Michigan State University (U.S.A).

McCormick, D. (1993). *Risk and Firm Growth: The Dilemma of Nairobi's Small-scale Manufacturers.* Institute of Development Studies, University of Nairobi.

McCormick, D. (1996), The Impact of Economic Reform on Entrepreneurial Activity: A Theoretical Framework for Analysing Small Enterprise, Journal of Eastern African Literary and Cultural Studies IDS- NAIROBI.

McCormick. (1998) *Gender in small Enterprise Development in Kenya: An Institutional Analysis,* Institute of Development Studies, University of Nairobi Kenya, 1998, pp.1-20.

McCormick, D. and Pedersen, P.O. (1996). *"Small Enterprises" Flexibility and networking in an African context.* Nairobi: Longhorn Kenya Ltd.

McCleland, D. (1961). *The Achieving Society,* Collier-McMillan Ltd, London.

McCleland, David C. (1961). *The Achieving Society,* Princeton: Von Norstrand.

McCormick, Dorothy.(1993. *Risk and Firm Growth: The Dilemma of Nairobi's Small – scale Manufacturers,* IDS.

National MSE(s) Baseline Survey.(1999). Central Bureau of Statistics, International Center for Economic Growth (ICEG) and K-Rep Holdings Ltd.

National Poverty Eradication Plan, February 1999, Kenya.

Pederden, P.O.and Dorothy McCormick. (1999). "Africa Business Systems in a Globalizing World," Journal of Modern African Studies, 37:1 (1999) p. 109 – 135 UK- Cambridge University Press.

Rasmussen, Jasper. (1992). *The Entrepreneurial Milieu: Enterprise Networks in Small Zimbabwean Town.* Department of Geography, Roskilde University and Centre for Development Research, Co-Penhagen.

Richter, N. (1993). *Entrepreneurs in a Disabling Environment,* Thesis University of Roskilde – Denmark.

Rosalind, Levacic. (1987). *Economic Policymaking.* Wheat's leaf Books, New Jersey.

Robert, F. Herbert and Albert, N. Link. "In search of the meaning of Entrepreneurship." Small Business Economics 1 (1989), 39 – 49, Kluwer Academic Publishers.

Ronald, A. Heifetz and Mary Linsky. (2002). *"A Survival Guide for Leaders,"* Harvard Business Review, June 2002, p.65 – 74.

Sessional Paper No. 2 of 1992 on *Small Enterprise and Jua Kali Development* in Kenya, March 1992.

Sessional Paper No.3 of 2004 on *Development of Micro and Small Enterprises for Wealth Creation and Employment Generation.* Republic of Kenya) ministry of labour and human resources Development.

Sexton, D.L and Smilor R.W. (1997). *Entrepreneurship 2000: The family business Dimension of Entrepreneurship,* pp. 243 – 266.

Scapens, R.W. (1990). "Researching Management Accounting Practice: The role of Case Study Methods, "University of Manchester.

Scott, E.C. (1986). *"Why more Women are becoming Entrepreneurs"* Journal of Small Business Management, October 1986, pp. 37 -44.

Schumpeter, J.A. (1934). *"The Theory of Economic Development,"* Harvard University Press, Cambridge.

Schultz, Theodore, W, (1975). *"The value of Ability to deal with Diequilibria",* Journal of Economic Literature, 13:827 – 46.

Suerrison, Arni. (1998). *Entrepreneurship and Industrialization in Kenya, Tanzania and Zimbabwe,* Research policy Institute, Jan. 18, 1988.

Theodore, Levitt. (2002). *Creativity is not enough: The Innovative Enterprise,* Harvard Business Review, August 2002, P. 137 – 145.

Venkataraman, S, and Joo-Heon, Le. (2000). *Aspiration level, Labour Market, Evaluation and the Decision to become an Entrepreneur.* The Darden School of Business Administration, University of Virginia.

Webber, A.M. (1992). *"Japanese Style Entrepreneurship"* Harvard Business Review, Jan – Feb 1992,pp.93 – 103.

Wickham, A.Philip.(1998). *Strategic Entrepreneurship: A Decision-Making Approach to New Venture Creation and Management,* PITMAN Publishing.

Zikmund, W.G (1988). *Business Research Methods.* The Dryden Press.

INDEX

www.ingramcontent.com/pod-product-compliance
Lightning Source LLC
Chambersburg PA
CBHW021714210326
41599CB00013B/1646